What people are saying

I wish I'd been taught this in school. It's life-changing stuff – not just for you, but for those around you. These are skills, once learnt and practised, that will unquestionably improve the quality of your life.

> – Tony Hawks MBE, TV and radio comedian and bestselling author, including *Round Ireland with a Fridge*

This book has so much to teach us all about building connections and understanding through the simple, but often neglected, act of listening – really listening – to other people. And to ourselves. At a time when so many of us have become isolated, with only a screen for company, the timing of this book could not be better. It is a tool box. Keep it close at hand and dip in often.

> – Jim Carter OBE and Imelda Staunton CBE, actors

'Why Weren't We Taught This at School?' is the right question. Knowing that behind all troublesome behavior we express, or experience with others, lurks an unmet need that is looking for satisfaction brings clarity to nearly every human interaction. And that is exactly what Alice Sheldon does in this aptly titled book. Anyone reading it will find their experience put in the context of need satisfaction along with a process for identifying and satisfying those needs. Recommended for everyone.

> – Harville Hendrix, PhD, and Helen LaKelly Hunt, PhD, co-authors of *Getting the Love You Want: A Guide for Couples*

From the world of business

Alice Sheldon's insightful book examines the obstacles that we commonly encounter in our interactions with others. Her solution is brilliant, easy to understand and applies with equal force in personal and professional contexts. This is an invaluable toolkit for honest, compassionate and effective communication.

> – Sharif Shivji QC, barrister specialising in commercial law

The ability to build and sustain relationships with a wide range of people is an essential skill in business in order to get things done. By using the tools outlined in this book, managers at all levels of seniority can foster the kind of environment in which people feel engaged and can give their best, finding creative and efficient solutions in seemingly intractable situations. A must-read book for 21st century leaders.

> – John Odell, director of one of the 'Big Four' professional services firms

At last Alice Sheldon has put her brilliant Needs Understanding approach into a book! It has been my go-to framework for helping leaders on 'how to have difficult conversations' for many years. Whilst Emotional Intelligence frameworks help with empathic awareness and even self-regulation, Needs Understanding goes further in providing a simple, practical, yet powerfully transformative approach to solve problems where no one loses out, relationships remain intact and everyone flourishes. This clear, practical, yet profound book will help you see relationship-building, creative strategising and problem-solving without compromise in a completely new light. Applying the concepts in *Why Weren't We Taught This at School?* is one of the most powerful things you can do to transform your relationships and contribute to a more healthy, joyful, sustainable world.

– Heather Monro, executive coach, Brightspace

Now, more than ever, we need to lean towards each other, developing more trusting and genuine relationships with work colleagues, with friends and with family members. This book is packed with personal stories, insightful examples and practical skills to demonstrate empathy and build collaborative solutions.

– Mark Pilkington, sales and marketing leader in the travel and leisure industry

A really accessible and engaging read, with lots of practical suggestions to enable improved outcomes and results for all parties. Alice's experience in this field really shows, and makes a clear case for the benefit of adopting Needs Understanding in both work and home environments.

– Matthew Wait, chief financial officer of a leading global education firm

This is one of the most impactful books I have read for many years. Simple lessons and practices that can change the way we engage with ourselves and with each other, and yet *Why Weren't We Taught This at School?* Instead we struggle and bumble through our lives not really understanding how things work. This book opens our eyes and gives us a manual on how to get our lives off the ground, and be the really wonderful human beings that we were born to be.

– Veronica Munro, international executive coach, author, and artist

From the world of education

This book is so beautifully written and reminds me of all the things I thought I knew, but somehow do not manage to keep live in my head at every interaction. I reflect on recent conversations when I 'should' have known better, and yet somehow got drawn into being less than my best self. Without judgement, and with huge compassion, Alice empathises with readers like me because she's been there too. I can see that this is a book I will want to return to again and again.

– Dr Belinda Hopkins, author of *The Restorative Classroom*
and director of Transforming Conflict

This is such a refreshing book. Alice wants us to understand ourselves, and how our needs impact our communication and relationships, and this oozes out of the book in such a skilful way. For anyone who works with humans of any age, or is a human, this book is transformational. My hope is that this is what the next generations will learn at school.

– Lily Horseman, chair, Forest Schools Association

Alice has written a book that is easy to read, describing simple strategies that are easy to apply. It makes you wonder why we don't all do this already! With every page, I found myself thinking, 'I must share this with…' This is a timely book, landing at a time when mental health issues are increasingly prominent and when we seem to be bombarded with disharmony and disagreement in the media. It should be essential reading for our political leaders.

– Adam Barber, head, Henleaze Junior School

A timely, compassionate and pragmatic reminder of the lessons which matter most; essential reading for all who teach and lead in schools, or wish they'd been taught differently themselves.

– Fionnuala Kennedy, head, Wimbledon High School

Alice Sheldon lives what she writes; this book is built on her thorough exploration of simple and powerful principles and tools, full of examples and insights of everyday life experiences. It is an art to be able to write in such a clear and structured form, easy to read and to concretely try out in our daily lives. A practical inspiration to make a difference in relationships with ourselves, with others and in the local and global political and economic structures we live in.

– Gabriele Grunt, co-founder of ECHT Communication and trainer for teacher and parent education

From the world of conflict resolution

A beautifully simple guide to the relationship skills we all so deeply need, but most of us don't know how to access. This book belongs firmly on the curriculum for creating a more peaceful world.

– Dr Scilla Elworthy, three times nominee for the Nobel Peace Prize and founder of the Business Plan for Peace

This book offers a rich analysis of compassionate and empathetic forms of communication. In a world so divided, devoting thought and care to transforming conflict and nurturing relationships seems more necessary than ever. The Needs Understanding framework is therefore a timely treasure trove.

– Nomisha Kurian, co-chair of the Cambridge Peace and Education Research Group

Why Weren't We Taught This at School? is an empathic and insightful guide to creating a world with less fear and more compassion. I found it to be easy to navigate, full of analogies with lots of tools to guide and bring clarity. As for 'needs glasses' – brilliant, everyone should have a pair!

> – Gina Lawrie, assessor with the Centre for Nonviolent Communication and co-creator of the NVC Dance Floors

Alice Sheldon's book is an essential guide for anyone who wants to contribute to a world where everyone matters. I spend my life seeking to 'be the change I want to see in the world', and this is a book which I'd put firmly on a reading list for life and especially for anyone who has influence over others.

> – Maria Arpa MBE, executive director of the Center for Nonviolent Communication and founding chair of the Centre for Peaceful Solutions

From the world of psychotherapy

A passionate, wise and authentic book with lessons that have clearly been lived and refined. The skills outlined are simple but never simplistic. A rich template for living a skilful life.

> – Malcolm Stern, co-founder of Alternatives, psychotherapist, and author

The ideas in this book are deeply transformational and it would serve humanity well if a copy were to find itself in everyone's hands. What an infinitely more connected and peaceful world we would live in if the relationship skills found within this treasure trove were integrated into the heart of our communication with one another. Written intelligently, with compassion and honesty. We couldn't wish for a more authentic guide.

> – Cheryl Garner, psychotherapist, Imago Relationship Therapist, and parenting coach

And from the world of myth and mermaids

Alice Sheldon has written a timely and much needed book about how to rethink the way we speak to each other. Full of sound advice and practical exercises, she unpacks ideas fundamental to our unconscious needs and actions. This is a book we all need as we go forward into complex, difficult times of climate crisis and a post-pandemic world. More than anything, this is a book about how to be skilful and compassionate about ourselves and others. A book for our time.

> – Monique Roffey, author of *The Mermaid of Black Conch* and winner of the Costa Book of the Year 2020

Why weren't we taught THIS at school?

The surprisingly simple secret to transforming life's challenges

ALICE SHELDON

First published in Great Britain by Practical Inspiration Publishing, 2021

© Alice Sheldon, 2021

The moral rights of the author have been asserted

ISBN   9781788602952   (print)
        9781788602945   (epub)
        9781788602938   (mobi)

Every effort has been made to trace copyright holders and to obtain their permission for the use of copyright material. The publisher apologizes for any errors or omissions and would be grateful if notified of any corrections that should be incorporated in future reprints or editions of this book.

Cover and interior graphic design: Eduardo Iturralde

Illustrations: Lily Horseman

Practical Inspiration
Publishing

MIX
Paper from
responsible sources
FSC   FSC® C013604
www.fsc.org

For Anna, light of my life

Contents

Introduction

Why weren't we taught this at school?

When you think back to your school days, what were the lessons you learned? Years later, many of us can remember our times tables, and yet feel lost when it comes to making sense of ourselves and others. We studied Maths and English, Science and Art, but most of us weren't equipped with a toolkit for making tricky decisions, handling our feelings, or building the kinds of relationships in which everyone thrives.

This has left us with an approach to life that offers mixed results. Sometimes everything clicks into place: our decisions flow easily and we're able to get on with the people around us without any effort. But at other times, we find ourselves feeling frustrated or unsure. We replay conversations over and over in our heads, wishing we had said things differently. We go back and forth endlessly when we're trying to make a difficult decision. We long to get through just one week without anyone in our families or workplaces quarrelling, shouting, or sulking. Or we feel as though life is slipping away from us without our achieving what we want.

It's as though we're missing some of the essential pages of life's instruction manual. A guide that would show us how to tap into what's important so that we can create the change we desire. A framework for overcoming challenges more simply. And a way of making sense of the world so that life becomes easier to enjoy.

That's what Needs Understanding offers us. It's a powerful way of creating relationships in which everyone flourishes and of solving problems where no one loses out. You can use it across the board – at home, at work, and with your friends and associates. Not only is it transformational but it's also deeply practical. It's simple enough that you can learn the core principles in an hour or two and make an immediate difference to your daily life, or use it as a quick fix when you're dealing with a tricky situation. And it's profound enough to offer a way of transforming long-held patterns of thinking that hold you back from living life to the full. What's more, it works even if you're the only one who knows about it; you don't have to bring your partner, colleagues, or friends on board as well.

It's based on one core idea: that everything we say or do is an attempt to meet our underlying human needs – needs like choice, being heard, creativity, or authenticity. When we look at the world through the lens of needs, we discover exciting new solutions to our difficulties. Previously inexplicable behaviour starts to make sense, life feels simpler, and the world becomes a friendlier place in which we can achieve what we want.

Needs Understanding is based on the outlook that creating change in your personal life is one of the most powerful things you can do to affect the world more widely as well as to live more happily. At the same time, it works well alongside an appreciation of how the systems in our culture distribute power and resources unevenly, recognising the social, political, and economic factors that can get in the way of achieving our potential in life. This makes it a powerful tool for creating the social change that can lead to a world in which everyone's needs are held with care.

Needs Understanding and me

I've been sharing the principles of Needs Understanding with organisations, groups, and individuals for many years now. After graduating with an MA in Psychology and Neurophysiology, I worked as a teacher and later as a barrister. Throughout my teens and twenties I lived with an increasing level of self-doubt and despair, and eventually hit rock bottom. My relationships were a mess, I'd lost any sense of purpose, and I couldn't see the point of carrying on.

My transformation from a person who was in deep depression, convinced of her complete inability to 'do relationships', feel joy, or live a meaningful life, to how I see myself today – confident in my capacity for bringing vitality to myself and others – was a slow process. Through it all, I never lost my curiosity. How could people, regardless of their beliefs or status in society, work together to create a world that works for everyone who inhabits the planet and indeed the planet itself? And how could I play my part in this?

Two life-changing influences helped me to see the possibility of another way of living.

The first was psychotherapy. This challenged me to view my inner struggles with empathy. It taught me to use my past experiences as a practical key for unlocking a different future. I learned how to relate to myself and other people, with a focus on authentic connection. All of these insights are core to Needs Understanding.

The second influence was the work of Marshall Rosenberg, who developed the concept of Nonviolent Communication

(NVC) from the 1960s onwards. It was in his teachings that I first came across the idea of shared human needs as an explanation for why we behave as we do, an outlook that sits at the heart of Needs Understanding. Sadly, I missed doing any training with Marshall before he stepped back from teaching, so I never met him. I remain profoundly grateful to him for the body of work that he left, and to all those from whom I have learned NVC over the years.

How this book works

In the next chapter we'll explore more about Needs Understanding and how it may be helpful to you. You'll also be introduced to its four skill areas:

- **Listen with empathy:** how to recognise ten unhelpful ways of listening that you might not be aware of, and how to listen so that you create connection instead.

- **Understand yourself with compassion:** how to make sense of yourself and the 'fingerprint needs' that drive you so that you can navigate difficult situations more easily and productively.

- **Speak to be heard:** how to communicate with people in a way that makes your message most likely to get through.

- **Act with care for everyone's needs:** how to 'walk around the mountain' and find paths through challenging problems, arriving at solutions that work for everyone.

While I've written the book in the order that I find makes most sense for learning the concepts from scratch, please feel free to jump around the chapters in whatever way supports you best. You'll find Pause Boxes throughout that give you opportunities for reflection and to try out the ideas. If you're the kind of person who likes regular break-out moments to think about what you're learning, you may find that they suit you, while if you prefer to read on without stopping the flow, they could get in your way. The book is designed to make sense whether you take part in them or not.

To make the ideas behind this way of thinking easier to understand, I've included a range of stories about people who've put Needs Understanding into practice in their own lives. The stories are a mix of true and fictional, and I've changed the names and details to protect people's privacy. Also, because this is a book and not a video or film, I've had to represent the communication between the characters with words; in reality, we express many of our thoughts and feelings through gestures, tone of voice, and body language, which are just as important. And, in some cases, I've compressed the dialogue so that it appears as if a transformation took place over a short period of time when in reality it took longer to happen.

I'm excited to share Needs Understanding with you, and curious to see whether at the end of the book you share my key question. Given that this is such a simple approach, with such far-reaching consequences for our individual lives and our divided world, why weren't we taught it at school?

Chapter 1

The surprisingly simple secret

Understanding the world through the lens of needs

Right at the heart of Needs Understanding are two core principles that can hold an extraordinary power to help in all areas of life and work. Whether you want to understand yourself more fully, transform the way you relate to other people, or make your own unique contribution to a better world, these principles are key. We'll start exploring them in this first chapter, and we'll keep coming back to them throughout the book.

- Principle 1: Our behaviour is always an attempt to meet our needs.

- Principle 2: Our world works best when our chosen strategies take care of everyone's needs.

What do I mean when I talk about needs? We have survival needs such as food, water, shelter, and warmth. Then there are mental, emotional, and spiritual needs, such as learning, freedom, love, connection, and beauty. In short, needs are what human beings require in order to thrive as well as to survive. They're something that we all share.

To help you, here's a list of universal human needs broken down into different groups; you can find it again at the end of the book so it's always easy to reference, and you can also download a 'print out and keep' copy at www.needs-understanding.com.

LIST OF NEEDS

Physical Needs
Air
Food
Health
Light
Movement
Rest
Shelter
Touch
Water

Security
Emotional safety
Peace of mind
Physical safety
Protection
Stability

Freedom
Autonomy
Choice
Ease
Independence
Responsibility
Space

To Matter
Acceptance
Acknowledgement
Care
Compassion
Consideration
Empathy
Recognition
Respect
To be heard
To be seen
Trust
Understanding

Play / Leisure
Fun
Humour
Joy
Pleasure
Rejuvenation
Relaxation

Understanding
Awareness
Clarity

Discovery
Learning
Stimulation

Connection
Affection
Appreciation
Attention
Closeness
Companionship
Contact
Harmony
Intimacy
Love
Nurture
Sexual expression
Tenderness
Warmth

Community
Belonging
Communication
Cooperation
Equality
Inclusion
Mutuality
Participation
Partnership
Self-expression
Sharing
Support
Tolerance

Sense of Self
Agency
Authenticity

Competence
Dignity
Effectiveness
Empowerment
Growth
Healing
Honesty
Integrity
Knowing I'm enough
Mattering to myself
Self-acceptance
Self-care
Self-realisation

Meaning
Aliveness
Challenge
Consciousness
Contribution
Creativity
Exploration
Integration
Purpose

Transcendence
Beauty
Celebration
Communion
Faith
Flow
Hope
Inspiration
Mourning
Mystery
Peace
Presence

Everyone groups needs in slightly different ways. If you find yourself identifying needs that don't appear on my list, or if some of the groupings don't mean much to you, please feel free to alter it. The purpose of the list at this stage is to invite you to think about the full range of human needs, many of which we aren't conscious of in our day-to-day lives. If you're printing out a copy, you might like to stick it on your fridge or somewhere you can see it easily so that the needs become familiar.

PAUSE BOX

(First, a reminder that the book still makes sense if you choose to skip over the Pause Boxes or come back to them later.)

Become familiar with needs

Have to hand: the list of needs.

This is an opportunity to become familiar with the needs on the list.

Read slowly through the list of needs, noticing any feelings that come up. Choose one need that jumps out at you for any reason.

Reflect: why did I choose this need?

You might like to think about where the need shows up in your life today, and whether you recognise it from your past. Is it one that particularly matters to you, or that you're lacking in your life at the moment? Take a few moments to explore its significance to you.

How our needs influence our behaviour

Let's dive into an example of a situation from my own life, which I'll use to illustrate why needs are fundamental to the way we think and behave. I've chosen a conversation between me and my daughter Katy (I've changed her name). Although I'm using a parenting example in this first chapter, the same principles can be applied in similar ways in all sorts of other situations at home and at work.

When my daughter was six, her favourite thing in the world at weekends was to stay at home and play endless games with her toy people. I enjoyed joining in because it was a delight to be with her, but after a while I'd long to get out of the house and do something different. As a single mum with no one else at home to look after her, my strategy was to agree with her that we'd have some time playing before we'd visit the local café. But whenever the moment came for going out, the same thing would happen. She'd refuse to leave her toys, and the situation would descend into me shouting, pleading, or bribing her to do what I wanted. Either we'd go to the café with her feeling upset and angry, or we'd stay at home and I'd feel resentful and crazy with frustration.

PAUSE BOX

Explore how behaviour links to needs

Have to hand: the list of needs, and a pen and paper.

This is an opportunity to reflect on how our behaviour can be understood as an attempt to meet our needs.

Divide a piece of paper in two, with each side having its own heading: 'My needs' and 'Katy's needs'. Now turn to the list of needs.

1. Think about me. Have a go at guessing which needs lay beneath my desire to go to the café and jot them down. You might start with a need for stimulation, for example.

2. Then think about Katy. Have a go at guessing what her needs might have been, and jot them down. Perhaps you might include a need for fun, for example.

Note the word 'guess'. There are no rights or wrongs – we can never know for sure because we each experience the world differently.

Let's imagine that, given the repetitive nature of the scenario, I want to find a different way for next weekend. What could I do differently? I can start by putting on a pair of 'needs glasses' and looking at the situation through the lens of needs. Now I can ask myself what I need in this scenario – what is it that really matters to me here? When I think about going to the café, those of my needs that jump out most strongly are:

- *aliveness*: a longing to feel full of energy and possibility;

- *connection*: a desire to enjoy being together with my daughter; and

- *to matter*: this is less obvious, and I'll come back to it in a moment.

What about Katy? What are her needs, and what role do they play in her refusal to go out? Here are my best guesses:

- *choice*: this is a huge need for most children as they have so much less autonomy than adults;

- *to be heard*: she wants me to fully understand what's important to her; and

- *fun*: she's loving playing with her toy people and doesn't want to stop.

You might like to try putting yourself in the same situation as me. Would your needs be different from mine, or the same? Different people's needs can vary even in the same situation because we each have our own individual responses.

So how does this way of understanding the situation help? Let's use the example of Katy and me to explore the four skill areas of Needs Understanding, which correspond to the four parts of this book.

The four skill areas of Needs Understanding

The four skill areas are tools that can help you to understand yourself and others. They offer ways of making the changes you want so that you can thrive personally and professionally, and make a difference to the world around you. The skill areas flow from the two core principles: our behaviour is always an attempt to meet our needs, and our world works best when our chosen strategies take care of everyone's needs.

These are the skill areas:

1. Listen with empathy

2. Understand yourself with compassion

3. Speak to be heard

4. Act with care for everyone's needs

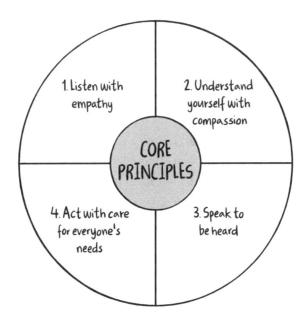

In this first chapter, I'll offer an overview of each of the four skills to give you a flavour of what is to come. In the rest of the book, we'll look at them in much more detail.

1. Listen with empathy (Part One)

When I look through a lens which tells me that everything my daughter does is an attempt to meet her needs, I have a new context for understanding the situation, and this context helps me to empathise with her. Without this awareness, I might try reasoning instead. 'We agreed to go out after we'd had some time playing, remember?' or 'But you love going to the café! I can buy you one of those gingerbread men you like.' If this worked, both in terms of gaining the results I wanted *and* maintaining a good relationship with her, I might carry on. However, as this isn't the case, I could try changing my thinking. With my needs glasses on I don't need to reason, argue, or persuade. Instead, I can begin by letting her know that I want to understand her world. 'It looks as though you're having a lot of fun playing here,' or 'It sounds as if *you'd* like to decide whether we go out.'

Empathising with someone can have a profoundly connecting effect, so why don't we do it more often? It can sometimes be because we worry that we'll have to give up on our own needs. We're afraid that we'll have to agree to what the other person wants and lose what's important to us. In this case, I might stay at home and play. My longed-for trip to the café, with its promise of aliveness, would be no more.

And yet this isn't the Needs Understanding basis of empathy. By empathising with my daughter, I'm recognising that all she's trying to do is to meet her needs for fun, choice, and to be heard. The problem is that she's meeting them in a way that doesn't work for me, because I have my own needs as well. By acknowledging what's going on for her, I'm likely not only to keep the connection between us alive, but also to find a mutually agreeable solution – one that meets both of our needs.

In Part One of the book we'll explore how to listen so that you can build connection rather than block it, and how you can discover and express empathy.

2. Understand yourself with compassion (Part Two)

What's going on with me when I find Katy's behaviour so frustrating? For a start, I have plenty of judgemental thoughts in my head. It's all her fault: 'You've had all morning playing, and now I want to do something I enjoy you're refusing to go out. You're spoiling our lovely day together!' Or it's all my fault: 'She's only six, of course she can't stick to plans. I'm such a bad mother, being so impatient with her. Other parents would deal with this in a much kinder way – why can't I be more like them?'

However, with my needs glasses on, I can become curious about my needs rather than stumbling around in a futile circle of blame. Understanding myself with compassion removes notions of fault: 'I'm blaming myself and feeling frustrated with Katy because I'm desperate for some aliveness after our morning at home. And I love her and want it to be easier to spend time together without either of us spiralling into a bad mood.' Now I'm better able to make sense of my frustration, which lays the groundwork for me to do things differently.

Many people find this second skill area of Needs Understanding to be both the most transformational, and also the hardest to learn. We'll explore it in Part Two.

3. Speak to be heard (Part Three)

When we speak, we want to be heard. And yet so often in our most important relationships or when we're dealing with those who can help us to achieve what we want, we find it hard to get people to listen. This can leave us feeling frustrated and resentful, and we end up taking these emotions out on them. On the other hand, if we can speak so we're likely to be heard and understood, our words will come across powerfully – we just have to know *when* and *how* to express ourselves so this happens.

In terms of *when*, the more the other person experiences being heard for their needs first, the readier they are to hear what's going on for us. If we find ourselves becoming blocked in difficult conversations, it's usually because each of us is trying to make the other one hear what we're saying, and neither person has the sense that they're being listened to. Taking the situation with my daughter, if I can empathise with her needs first, she'll know that I understand what's troubling her about going out. This makes it more likely that she'll be open to hearing what matters to me as well.

In terms of *how* to express myself, Katy will be more likely to understand where I'm coming from if I talk about my needs rather than arguing my case for going out. So, after empathising with her, I might say: 'And for me, I'm wanting to fill up on what I need so I have lots of energy for the rest of the day.' There's no guilt tripping or manipulation here, only clarity and self-responsibility. My aim is to create more connection with my daughter through a greater mutual understanding.

Speaking to be heard is a highly practical tool, which we'll look at in Part Three. It includes talking about needs rather than strategies, observations rather than evaluations, and requests rather than demands.

4. Act with care for everyone's needs (Part Four)

When we come up against a disagreement with someone, we tend to leap straight from problem to solution:

We might attempt to persuade the other person with reason and logic, we might threaten them with the consequences of not doing what we want, or we might try and manipulate them to shift to our way of seeing things. The drawback with these approaches is that each person then becomes entrenched in their own position, locked into a win–lose pattern in which one gets what they want and the other gives way.

In the case of my daughter and me, my original solution was that we'd have a certain amount of time playing and then go to the café. This seemed like a workable option to me, but on closer reflection it was probably never going to succeed. Given that Katy didn't want to go out in the first place, it was unlikely that she'd ever agree to it in practice. The most likely scenario was what actually happened: she agreed to the extra time playing and then still refused to leave the house. This leaping straight from problem to practical solution was an understandable course for me to take, because I wanted to instantly rid myself of the irritation I felt. But it produced an outcome that left me feeling even more frustrated, and with less of the connection I longed for with Katy.

However, there's a different way of thinking about the problem, which is likely to be more productive. Rather than jumping straight to a solution, I can choose to look below the surface to understand both of our needs:

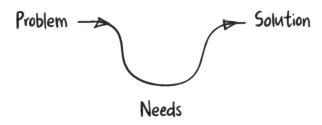

A solution that you come to via a consideration of both parties' needs is far more likely to work, and to enhance the relationship, than one that's based on a knee-jerk strategy. In Katy's and my case, I'm now looking for something that meets her needs for choice, fun, and being heard, as well as my needs for aliveness, connection, and mattering. After empathising with her so that she knows she's been heard, I might suggest we go out but take her toys with us. If she says 'no', I can ask her what she could think of that would give her fun and me some aliveness. Even young children are remarkably resourceful in coming up with strategies that suit everyone, and in giving her the option I'm also meeting her need for choice.

Of course, it's possible that Katy will still refuse to go out and that, try as I might, I may not be able to find a way of staying in that meets my need for aliveness. If that happens I could decide to set a boundary, which in Needs Understanding terms is loving rather than punitive. 'I know you want to stay here and carry on playing, and if we do that all day I'll not be able to look after what I need as well. I can't find a way that works for us both and so I'm going to insist that we go out even though I know you don't want to.' I'm describing what I'm doing, letting my daughter know that I understand my solution doesn't work for her. I'm also not feeling as angry with her as I might if I wasn't aware of my needs. We're not arguing about the strategy (whether or not we go out), but have moved to considering the needs involved.

When applying this fourth skill area, it can be helpful to use the analogy of a cooking pot. Instead of a rigid line travelling from problem straight to solution, you're putting everyone's needs into the pot and seeing what comes out at the end.

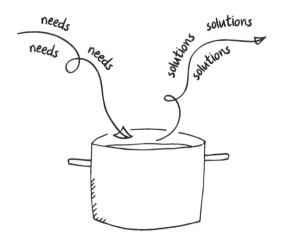

I like the idea of the cooking pot because it illustrates what's effective about needs-based problem-solving.

- It's unique to each situation – every dish that comes out of the pot is different depending on the ingredients (the needs) and how they're combined (recognised and handled).

- It's creative, recognising that there's usually a huge number of strategies to deal with a problem, rather than just one.

- It produces a nourishing outcome that lasts for the long term, rather than a fast-food fix that leaves you feeling empty after a while.

- It takes a bit more time than jumping to a solution, but it's worth it because it's so much more tasty and satisfying.

Acting with care for everyone's needs is something that we'll explore in Part Four.

Replacing strategies with needs

To come to a solution that acknowledges both parties' needs involves pausing and reflecting. It can also require a change to your habitual approach. The key is to be as ready as you can to let go of your preferred strategy – the one you might have leapt to straightaway before – and instead to keep a firm hold on the needs underneath. It's the opposite of what many of us are used to doing.

We're incredibly attached to some of our strategies. For instance, when a friend of mine discovered Needs Understanding, she looked back at a situation in her past and saw it in a very different light. A few years ago, when her company was growing and she was expanding her work team, she thought she had found the perfect recruit. The problem was that he lived four hundred miles away in rural Scotland, and she thought it was important that all her team members were located in one place. She asked him if he would consider moving, but although he would have loved to take the job – it would have been transformational for him – he wouldn't because he loved the area so much. His fixation on staying put was a strategy based on his needs for freedom and beauty. Likewise, my friend's suggestion that he move down was based on her requirements for certainty and connection. When she reflects back on the situation now, she wonders what creative options could have come out if she'd known how to put all the needs in the pot.

When we believe that there's only one solution to a problem between us and someone else, it's often a warning sign that we've forgotten to think about the underlying needs at play. There's usually a whole range of solutions available to us for that issue in that moment, even if we can't see them at first. Just as every meal that comes out of the pot is different depending on what goes in, so there's a rich array of potential options that will best meet all of the needs involved.

What's more, because we're not used to distinguishing between needs and strategies, we can become scared of letting go of our preferred solution. We're attached to it, thinking that it represents our needs. Instead, we can say, 'I'm absolutely not going to let go of my needs. And, for just ten minutes, I'm going to pretend that I could solve this problem in a different way.' This is a switch of attachments, which can be quite difficult at first; when we let go of one thing and allow something else to become more important, it feels strange – even scary and wrong. The concept is simple but the habit is hard to shift. We'll be returning to this in Part Four (Act with care for everyone's needs).

Fingerprint needs

Earlier in the chapter, one of the needs I identified for myself in my conversation with my daughter was my need 'to matter'. When I think about why this was important to me, it comes down to my upbringing. Growing up, I experienced 'not mattering' over and over again, with the result that I have a chronically unmet need to know that I matter. This means that whenever the way that someone behaves touches on my need to matter, I find myself catapulted back to my childhood. If I'm not mindful that mattering is one of my needs, I'll start feeling and behaving like my five-year-old self rather than a rational adult. In the example of Katy and me, it's clearly not her responsibility to make me feel that I matter, and I'm at risk of dumping my issue onto her if I don't take care of the need myself.

I call my need to matter a 'fingerprint need', and each of us typically has a handful – around two to five. We'll look at them in more detail later on, but for now it's worth knowing that they're usually central to understanding some of the behaviours and attitudes that we most want to change in ourselves. From the person in our team whom we just can't get on with, to the times when we're crippled with self-doubt, to the flare of anger when we row with a loved one – a lack of understanding of our fingerprint needs can underlie many of our difficulties in navigating life.

Our fingerprint needs are usually related to how well (or not) our caregivers met our needs when we were children, regardless of how loving a home we may have grown up in. When something in our adult world touches on one of them, it becomes an overriding priority for us to grab onto whatever it is that we're not getting. We lurch into the same survival mode in which we lived when we were three or four years old and depended on our caregivers for everything. The situations in which we overreact to a fingerprint need not being met are also those that tend to cause us the most issues in our close relationships.

What are your fingerprint needs? A helpful way to identify them is to think about situations in which you've found yourself having a disproportionate reaction to something that someone said or did. You thought to yourself afterwards, 'Why on earth did I do that?' For instance, you're driving along and another car shoots out of a side road with no warning, swerving in front of you. Of course, you feel shock and irritation. But if you find yourself slamming your foot on the accelerator and charging after the car while yelling and honking your horn, that's probably a reaction to an unmet fingerprint need.

Fingerprint needs can bring up deep emotions. When we explore them in a training session there's often someone who's moved to tears. Suddenly it makes sense to them, for instance, why they feel smaller than their colleagues every time they walk into the office, and it's a release. Our needs give us powerful explanations for our behaviour, but only when we know what they are. We'll look at how to find our own needs when we come to Part Two (Understand yourself with compassion).

But what about…?

From my experience of working with people on this, I'm guessing that you may have some challenging questions, and even objections, by now. Rather than leave them hanging, I'll share what I usually find to be the main ones together with my answers.

Sometimes people do bad things. Are you asking me to excuse them by understanding their needs?

In short, no. Developing a compassionate, needs-based understanding of someone's behaviour doesn't mean that you have to accept or agree with it. However, you can still look at the person through needs glasses. Striving to understand why they act the way they do gives you a greater chance of coming up with constructive solutions than if you leap straight to judging them.

I'm so angry/anxious/upset/numb [delete as appropriate] that I can't stop myself from blaming other people – I find it impossible to see their needs

I'm with you! Often the situations we most want to improve are those in which we feel most triggered by another person's behaviour. We want to fix that recurring argument with our partner, stop our boss from intimidating us, or get through to our child that their behaviour isn't acceptable. But sometimes it's just too difficult to work with these situations at first, because when we feel angry and upset (or even numb) we're a bit like a robot operating in 'react' mode. You might like to park these aims for now so as to avoid feeling discouraged if you don't make headway with them immediately, and turn your attention to scenarios that you feel curious about instead. For many of us that's an easier way to begin, while all the time knowing that we can use the same techniques to tackle our hardest problems later on when we have had more practice.

I'm not sure that I like the word 'needs'

You might find the word has connotations of 'neediness' for you, hinting at dependence or weakness. You're not alone. I haven't yet found a better word that works for everyone, so I continue to use 'needs'. If it gets in the way for you, feel free to use an alternative that you prefer. Suggestions include: 'values', 'things that are important to me', and 'things I love'.

Can I use Needs Understanding on my own?

Yes! Part of the beauty of the framework is that it doesn't require anyone else but you to know its principles or how to use the tools. When you listen fully to others, work out what's going on for yourself with compassion, and speak in ways that make it likely you'll be understood, you're able to create connections with people who have no knowledge of it. You don't need to persuade your spouse, boss, or colleagues to learn it. What's more, when you use it on a regular basis, you may find that your relationships shift in a surprising way, almost as if it were the other people who were doing the changing.

Surely we can't always meet everyone's needs?

That's right, we can't. That's why Part Four is called 'Act *with care for* everyone's needs' not 'Act *to meet* everyone's needs'. The idea is that we make sure that all needs matter to us, even if we can't find a solution that works across the board. That said, as you practise Needs Understanding more and more, you may be surprised by how often you can achieve an outcome that does meet everyone's needs.

Once you move your focus away from your preferred strategy for solving problems to understanding the underlying needs at play, it's surprising how many creative solutions you can find. Sometimes a strategy that would have been unacceptable to everyone before becomes a viable way forward; because of the sense of mutual understanding and care, we and they can happily shift position. Even when you can't find a mutually acceptable option and end up with one that meets one person's needs and not another's, the act of understanding and empathising with the other person can strengthen your relationship with them. This can have a long-term benefit.

The list of needs is far too long – I'll never remember it

It can seem that way when you first look at it. There are a few things that have helped me with this.

Firstly, it's a finite list. Human nature doesn't change so much that there will be more needs added to it. Given how complex we are, I like the simplicity of framing all the things we need to survive and thrive on a single piece of A4 paper.

Secondly, as you become used to looking at the world through the lens of needs, you'll start to recognise the ones that show up repeatedly in your life. Some of them will be your fingerprint needs. Most of us have only a handful of these, and another handful of others that we come to recognise in day-to-day situations – they're the ones you can focus on.

And thirdly, please don't feel that you need to memorise the list or keep going back to it. As you learn to look at yourself and others in new ways, you'll increasingly distinguish between strategies and needs. The list is only there as a reference point to help you to find the needs at play in a situation, and to notice the ones that recur.

This is far too much to think about

Yes, it can be – at the beginning at least. So I have two suggestions.

Firstly, think about situations in the past (or ones in the future that you're worried about) and consider how Needs Understanding applies to them. If the scenario is a recurring one, you can practise handling it differently next time. The main thing is that it's not a 'live' situation for you now, so you're only mentally rehearsing how you'd deal with it. Also, consider choosing a situation in which the emotional stakes are not too high; low or medium level is often best to start with.

Secondly, you can choose a particular skill to practise, and focus only on that. For instance, you could start by learning to listen empathically when someone speaks to you (Part One); or by discovering your own fingerprint needs and spotting them in day-to-day scenarios (Part Two). You could try altering how you express your feelings to people (Part Three); or practise using the language of collaborative problem-solving (Part Four). Please feel free to discover what works best for you on your learning journey, taking what you like and find useful, and leaving the rest behind.

PAUSE BOX

Find a way to remember about needs

Have to hand: the list of needs.

Keep this book somewhere to hand, with a bookmark in the list of needs. Better still, print out the list by going to www.needs-understanding.com and stick it somewhere you can see it easily, like the fridge door.

When the list catches your eye, take a moment to focus on how you're feeling. Then scan the list to see which needs are behind what's going on for you.

Do the same for anyone else in the room around you by guessing what's up for them.

If you only take one thing from this chapter...

- Human behaviour is always an attempt to meet our needs.

And if you take a few more...

- The secret to happier and more productive relationships is to listen with empathy, understand yourself with compassion, speak to be heard, and act with care for everyone's needs.

- When you avoid leaping directly from problem to strategy, and instead consider everyone's needs, you're likely to come up with better solutions.

- Unmet fingerprint needs can explain many of your hardest or recurring conflicts.

- You can achieve transformational results even if you're the only person in a relationship who's practising Needs Understanding.

Listen with EMPATHY

Part One

This section focuses on learning to listen empathically. Many of us don't realise that the way we're used to listening can be a major block to developing fruitful connections in our relationships. When we listen with empathy instead, our conversations are more likely to generate mutual understanding, and to give us ways forward that fulfil all of our needs.

Chapter 2

How not to listen: ten things we say that can alienate people

- Ways of listening that block connection
- Help – I'm a terrible listener!
- Questions to help you explore your listening

Chapter 3

How to listen: tools for building empathy and connection

- How is listening with empathy helpful?
- What exactly is empathy?
- How can we learn to be more empathic?
  - How to be: develop an empathic attitude
  - What to say: find your authentic empathy language
- From empathy to action
- Some questions you may have about empathy

Chapter 2

How not to listen

Ten things we say that can alienate people

'Hmmm, this looks a bit worrying,' the doctor said. 'I'm going to refer you for a scan straightaway. You'll receive an appointment within two weeks.'

My stomach lurched. Here was my doctor telling me that the patch of skin on my breast might not be dermatitis after all, but a possible sign of cancer. Taking a couple of deep breaths, I focused on the office, the chair, the computer – anything that would help me to keep the panic from rising inside me.

When I arrived home after the appointment, I thought about what would make me feel better, and decided that I wanted to talk through my concerns. So I voiced my worries to a few friends, work colleagues, and family members. When I look back on those conversations, I'm convinced that each person I spoke with wanted to give me all the care and support they could. However, the extent to which that support got through to me varied immensely from person to person.

Where did the difference lie? It was in what they said in response to my news. Here are some of the reactions that didn't help me.

'Oh, I know all about cancer scares – I've had five scans myself in the last three years!'

'Two weeks is far too long to wait for an urgent scan. You should ring the clinic tomorrow and ask to be pushed up the list!'

'Try not to worry, I'm sure it's nothing.'

Why did I find these unhelpful? Because I wasn't ready to learn from my friend's experience of false cancer scares; I didn't want unasked-for advice about chasing my appointment; and when I was told not to worry, I didn't feel reassured, only unheard.

On the other hand, here are some of the reactions that did help me.

'Oh, that sounds pretty scary. How are you feeling about it?'

'I'm here to talk any time you want, but there's no pressure from my end to be in touch.'

'If you'd like me to come to the appointment with you I'll make sure I can.'

What felt supportive about these? Having a colleague acknowledge that I might be afraid, and then ask me how I felt, gave me licence to share some of my real worries. The suggestion from my brother that I get in touch, but only if I wanted to, meant that I knew I could call him while also being under no obligation to update or reassure him. And the offer from my best friend to come to the appointment with me, at the end of a conversation full of empathy and understanding, let me know that she understood what a big deal it was.

PAUSE BOX

Explore what it means to feel heard

Have to hand: a pen and paper.

Remember or imagine a time when you felt upset or angry. You wanted support and talked to a friend or family member, but didn't feel heard or understood.

Take a moment to note what the other person said or did that made you feel unheard. Examples might be, 'She kept checking her phone,' or 'He jumped straight in with his ideas about how to fix things before he'd listened to me.'

Now reverse the situation. This time you were still upset or angry, but when you sought support you felt as if you'd been understood. Note down what the other person said or did to make you feel that way. You might come up with something like, 'He kept really good eye contact,' or 'She made it clear she was happy to listen until I'd finished.'

Keep in mind what you've discovered about feeling heard and unheard as you read more about habitual listening and empathic listening below.

You might recognise this variety of reactions from your own experiences, both as recipient and giver. The first group – the reactions that didn't help me – are habitual listening responses. They represent patterns of thinking that we may have fallen into over the years, and they're mainly unconscious, in that we don't realise we're doing them. The problem they cause is that when someone tells us something and wants to be heard, these responses throw up a wall that blocks our connection with them.

Given that the first core principle of Needs Understanding is that all behaviour is an attempt to meet our needs, when we listen to someone we need to find a 'way in' to their experience that allows us to get in touch with what's important to them. This is what empathic listening does.

Ways of listening that block connection

Back to our habitual responses. Here are ten common, ingrained listening patterns, together with examples.

'I'm so scared about giving that big talk, I feel sick every time I think about it.'	
Advise	*'You should hire a coach to help you prepare.'*
Fix	*'Don't worry, it'll be over before you know it.'*
Explain or defend	*'I should have rehearsed it with you earlier!'*
Story tell	*'You're doing a talk – amazing! I went to a fabulous talk last month...'*
Fact find	*'When was the last time you gave a talk? Did you use slides?'*
One-up	*'That's nothing. I actually threw up the last time I did a presentation – I had to run from the stage!'*
Humour	*'You'll ace it – just remember to bring the right visuals this time!'*

Teach	*'Presentations are always awful – you just have to get through them and move on.'*
Ignore	**preoccupies self with thoughts of what advice to give next**
Sympathise	*'I've so been there. I hate that feeling of dread and not being able to sleep for days.'*

Can you recognise using any of these types of responses yourself? Let's explore the reasons why, when they're given as an initial reaction, they can be unhelpful if we want to respond supportively to the other person.

Advise: this is the classic response we so often fall into. In our haste to solve the problem, we assume that we know what's best and give advice accordingly. The result can be that the other person's feelings are silenced.

Fix: rather than exploring the speaker's feelings, we just want to make things better for them. This can mean that they shut down.

Explain or defend: this is when we take the comment as an attack on ourselves or someone else. Instead of hearing what the other person is saying, we leap into explanation or defence mode.

Story tell: in this response we steer away from listening to the speaker's experience so as to recount our own. The consequence is that they may feel ignored.

Fact find: asking questions that help us to understand the other person's story can work well. The problem arises when we hijack it by focusing on what we're interested in discussing, rather than listening to what they want to tell us. Sometimes the questions are the same in either case, but it's the intention with which they're asked that's different.

This means that they're also heard differently. One is an encouragement to carry on with the story being told, the other is a message that we want to follow our own agenda in the conversation.

One-up: this is when we share an example of how we've been similarly but more deeply affected by the same issue, and has the effect of drawing the attention back to us and shutting the speaker down.

Humour: we may joke when we're uncomfortable with difficult feelings in a conversation or when we're not sure how to handle it. The message is likely to come across to the other person that we want to move swiftly on from their problem.

Teach: we set ourselves up as an expert in the person's situation, rather than being interested in their own interpretation, or checking whether they'd like to hear our perspective.

Ignore: this can take the form of distracting ourselves, or of only thinking about what we want to say next. In either case, it keeps our attention firmly on ourselves.

Sympathise: people often ask about the difference between sympathy and empathy. The distinction I make is that sympathy is when we step into someone else's shoes *as ourselves* ('You must feel angry about losing all that money, because I would if it were me'). Empathy, on the other hand, is when we step into someone else's shoes *as them* ('What effect has losing all that money had on you?' – there's no assumption here, only an interest in exploring their world). When we sympathise, the person we're speaking with may not feel heard because we bring into the picture our preconception of what their situation feels like to them, rather than trying to learn what it's like from their viewpoint.

Here's another set of examples.

'Do you think I'm not spending enough time with my kids these days?'	
Advise	'Probably. Maybe you should consider working part-time.'
Fix	'I wouldn't worry. My parents never spent a lot of time with me and I turned out okay.'
Explain or defend	'I don't spend any more time with my kids than you do with yours.'
Story tell	'Yeah, a friend of mine at work had the same concern. She…'
Fact find	'How many clubs are they in? Do they do them each week?'
One-up	'You're doing well with yours! I've got so much on I never see my kids at all.'
Humour	'As long as you'd still recognise them in the street they'll be fine!'
Teach	'Spending quality time with our kids is the most important part of parenting.'
Ignore	*glances at phone*
Sympathise	'Hmmm. You must be worried they'll go off the rails if you don't spend more time with them.'

And a final one…

'It drives me mad when I'm always having to correct Jo's mistakes in her reports.'	
Advise	'If I were you, I'd make her use a spell check before she hands them in.'
Fix	'At least they're only minor errors. It could be worse.'

Explain or defend	'Maybe you're being a bit hard on her.'
Story tell	'Oh, I had someone like that who worked for me once...'
Fact find	'What are the reports about?'
One-up	'At least you got to leave on time. I had to stay until 10pm last night going through my team's reports.'
Humour	'It's a good job you're a superhero then!'
Teach	'You could treat this as an opportunity for her to learn about writing technique.'
Ignore	*thinks about own forthcoming report deadline*
Sympathise	'I know just how you feel. It's so annoying when people are too lazy to write something without making mistakes.'

Habitual listening can be categorised in many different ways, so use whatever grouping works for you. My aim with these examples is to demonstrate the multiple ways that we habitually – and unintentionally – listen, with the result that people can feel as if they haven't been heard.

Help – I'm a terrible listener!

When I first learned about this I assumed I must be an awful listener: 'I've been using these responses all my life!' I thought that I could see them showing up all over the place, and wondered if I could ever learn to do things differently. This isn't a unique reaction – when I work with people on this they recognise themselves again and again in the examples. So if you're in the same position, you're definitely not alone. Here are some ways of thinking about this that might help.

Firstly, one way to understand habitual responses is that sometimes they're just poorly timed. Advising, joking, or storytelling can be extremely helpful, but only *after* you've empathised with the other person and helped them to feel heard, understood, and accepted. You don't need to throw out all of your reactions, but you may want to consider the moment at which you give them.

Secondly, seeing how what we are doing is unhelpful but not yet knowing what to replace it with is a recognised stage of learning something new. Learning to empathise involves time and persistence, and it usually takes a while for it to become automatic.

Thirdly, your habitual responses are always an attempt to meet your needs. A woman returns home from work to see her husband putting dinner in the oven. 'I've had an awful day today,' she says. Her husband replies, 'There's half an hour before dinner's ready; why don't you have a lie down? I'll finish cooking while you relax.'

To his surprise, she looks disappointed. In his mind, he's finding a solution to her problem by inviting her to rest before dinner. His response is an attempt to meet his need to contribute to her, which he tries to do by offering her the solution that would have worked for him if it had been the other way round. What he hasn't understood is her underlying need to be heard. She experiences his response as a brushing aside of her feelings, made worse because she tells herself that she should be grateful for his offer. An empathic response from the husband might be to ask if she wants to talk more about her day, so he can understand why it was so tough. Or he might simply ask her what he could do that would help her most. Either way, he is trying to understand more directly what it is that she needs, rather than making assumptions based on what response he would have wanted in a reversed situation.

In all this, it can be helpful to remember that when we shut down a conversation it's often because there's too much going on for us at the same time. The husband may have had a stressful day himself, and not have the space to hear her problems. In that case he might answer, 'I'd like to know more. But right now I'm a bit full of my own stuff from the day I've had, and I'm not sure I can listen properly. How about we delay dinner, go for a run together, and then talk when we're sitting down?'

Questions to help you explore your listening

So what can you do instead? The first step is to identify those of your habitual listening patterns that get in the way of creating connection with others. If you can spot your most common responses, you can start to make choices about when they're serving you well and when they're not. The second step is to learn how to empathise instead, which is the subject of the next chapter.

The remainder of this chapter offers you four questions to explore habitual listening so that you can see how it shows up in your life, and where you might want to change how you respond.

Question 1: How comfortable are you with other people's feelings?

In habitual listening, we may try to steer the conversation away from how the speaker is feeling because we're not confident that we can handle their feelings. There are various possible reasons for this, and understanding them can help us to change how we listen. These reasons include the ones below.

We're uncomfortable with 'difficult' feelings, such as fear, pain, anger, and sadness. We may have grown up in a home in which they weren't handled with emotional maturity. This means we have little experience of managing them in a healthy way, so when they show up we use our habitual responses as a way of fixing or skirting round them.

We over-identify and become exhausted with the other person's feelings. Healthy empathy involves gaining a sense of what could be going on for someone, and may include experiencing something of what they're feeling, but if we over-identify with their issue we can become overwhelmed.

When we've learned how to take care of our own feelings, we can be more available to those around us. We'll explore various aspects of recognising and dealing with our own feelings in Part Two (Understand yourself with compassion).

We think that if we move the focus away from someone's feeling it will go away, believing that they will feel better as a result. This isn't the way it works. Feelings are absolutely key to sorting out problems, because (as we'll see later on) they give us helpful information about what isn't working now.

We assume that we know how to sort the problem out, which leads us to give advice so the other person can feel better. We may have something to share that could be useful at the right time, but until the other person knows that we've 'got' them, they're unlikely to be ready to hear our solution.

We have strong feelings ourselves, which means we can't understand what's going on for the speaker. It's hard to empathise with someone when we need empathy and understanding ourselves. This is where things often go wrong in our closest relationships – the ones in which there's a lot at stake. We need to take care of our own feelings first and then engage with the other, so that we can understand our different perspectives.

We take what the speaker is saying personally, which means that we can't hear their experience because we're too busy feeling ashamed or angry, or working out how to defend ourselves. Again, we need to notice and take care of our feelings so that we can keep our focus on what they're saying.

We doubt our capacity to listen, believing that we're 'bad at empathy' or 'can't do it right'. This takes us away from the speaker and back towards ourselves. As we'll see later, a helpful approach can be to cultivate an attitude of self-compassion; in this state, we can accept our self-judgemental thoughts and turn our attention back to where we want it to be – with the speaker.

Question 2: Where's your focus when you're listening?

In habitual listening, we take the focus of the conversation away from the person who's speaking, and bring it back to ourselves. Examples are when we're thinking about what we want to say next rather than fully listening, or when we jump in by sharing our own experiences too quickly. This means that the speaker feels as if they're not being heard. Spotting where the focus is can help us keep on track with empathic listening. We can ask ourselves: 'What do I say or do that will keep the focus on my friend, rather than take it away from them? Who's the star of the conversation?'

Question 3: What does the other person need from you?

Whenever someone talks to us about a problem, they're hoping for something from us, even if they (or we) don't know quite what it is. So if we're on the receiving end, before we say anything we may like to ask ourselves: 'What does this person need from me? Are they wanting me to listen fully to them? Are they wanting me to come up with a suggested way forward? Are they looking for my words or for my silence?' This can help us to keep the focus directed towards the other person and the most helpful response we can give.

Also, people don't always want or need empathy. If you call out a plumber because you have a problem with your central heating, you probably just want them to fix it. You're not interested in them offering you half an hour of empathy for your thermostat-related woes. There will be times when it's clear that the other person is looking for immediate ideas about what to do, and your advice or storytelling might be just what they need; they're not looking to be heard. As you practise tuning in to what people are looking for, you'll start to gain a better sense of what's needed and when.

Question 4: What might stop you using empathy?

It may be that you have concerns about empathy which mean that you keep using habitual listening, even when it isn't serving you well. Some of these might include the following.

Empathising with someone is usually more time-consuming than leaping in with an attempt at a quick-fix solution or opinion. However, once the other person knows that they've been heard, it takes much less time to find a way forward than it does to leapfrog the empathy part.

Empathy isn't just for those who think of themselves as good listeners. The skills of empathy that we'll cover in the next chapter are ones that can be learned whether you view yourself as an empathic person or not. And at its heart, empathy is simple, although it isn't always easy. Psychotherapist Sylvia Boorstein named one of her books *Don't Just Do Something, Sit There*.[1] It's about meditation, but the title expresses for me the

---

[1] Sylvia Boorstein, *Don't Just Do Something, Sit There: A Mindfulness Retreat* (San Francisco, Harper, 1996).

simplicity of empathy, which is that it only involves being fully present and listening to someone share what's going on for them. Sometimes we imagine it's difficult because we're so used to jumping in with our input that when we aren't 'doing' anything, we think we're not being empathic. However, you don't have to say or do anything specific to show that you're empathising, and having an empathic intention already gets you a long way there. We'll spend the whole of the next chapter getting to grips with putting empathy into practice and exploring how to empathise in a way that feels authentic for you.

You might think that if you empathise with someone you'll lose what's important to you. Sometimes we're afraid that if we open ourselves to hearing someone else's view with empathy and understanding, we're giving up on our own values or accepting actions we don't agree with. However, the Needs Understanding approach to empathy doesn't require you to agree with the other person in order to hear what's going on for them. You can hold on to your own needs and values, while choosing to focus fully on someone else at the same time. You might learn more about their perspective, but you can always return back to what's important to you.

Empathic listening can be just as powerful in writing, such as in emails and on social media, as it is in live conversation. In a Facebook group for authors, a friend posted about feeling stuck. She received multiple comments along the lines of, 'Have you tried this?' and 'Why don't you do that?' Regardless of how well-intentioned the messages were, it's especially easy to come across as uncaring in written form. By the time I spoke with my friend, she was feeling worse than ever about the block, and certainly not able to take on any of the proposed suggestions. What she was looking for was an initial empathic response, such as, 'What you're going through sounds really tough.' Having some sense that her worry had been heard could have opened her up to receiving the practical tips more easily.

In the next chapter we'll look in depth at how to listen with empathy, including ways of holding your focus on the speaker so that you allow them to own their feelings, and experience being truly heard.

If you only take one thing from this chapter…

- We habitually, and unintentionally, shut down other people's feelings when we dive in with our advice or opinions rather than listening fully first.

And if you take a few more…

- Our difficulties with listening empathically can be down to discomfort with our own feelings.

- If we can help the other person to feel heard and understood, it's more likely that they'll be open to hearing our perspective.

- Listening with empathy is the first step towards understanding someone's underlying needs, which in turn can lead to productive and fruitful conversations.

Chapter 3

How to listen

Tools for building empathy and connection

Having discovered how we unintentionally block our connections with other people, let's look at what we can do instead. We're going to explore various aspects of listening with understanding and insight, so that we can create relationships based on a mutual appreciation of one another's needs. Listening like this is a first step towards having a more fulfilling experience of our work and personal life.

With that in mind, we'll explore:

- how listening with empathy helps us;

- what empathy is;

- how we can learn to become more empathic; and

- common questions about using empathy.

How is listening with empathy helpful?

I first met Ian when he was feeling desperate because his daughter Lydia wanted to drop out of sixth form college. She was academically able and capable of thriving there, and he'd spent weeks unsuccessfully trying to 'get through' to her by laying out the arguments for staying on. This only led to more disagreements, and he didn't know what to do. After learning about listening with empathy, he decided to take a different approach. Instead of attempting to persuade Lydia, he resolved to prioritise his connection with her and simply listen to what she had to say. As they were driving in the car, Ian opened a conversation about how she felt about college – with no agenda to change her mind.

'It's really stressful,' Lydia said. 'There's so much work, and I have the long journey every day. The other kids are okay, but I don't have any proper friends there. It just feels like I'm wasting my time. I hate it.'

Ian listened, told her that he could see she felt unhappy, and left her space to carry on. By the end of their conversation he sensed that she'd picked up on the shift in his approach, and that she 'got' that Ian was genuinely interested in hearing her views. He realised that having a good relationship with Lydia was far more important to him than whether or not she went to college, and this change in energy brought with it a level of open-mindedness about her future options.

In the end, with her father's support, Lydia left college and got a job. Six months later, she decided she wanted to return to do her A levels – a decision she made on her own terms. Other parents might have made a different choice about what they wanted for their child and how to intervene, but the point is that approaching the situation with empathy can open up fresh possibilities and shift stagnant problems. Five years on, Ian credits their conversation in the car with the start of the amazing relationship that he and Lydia enjoy today.

Ian's story also highlights two reasons why empathy is helpful when resolving difficult issues.

Firstly, it helps you to create a quality of connection that enriches your relationships and feels good. Whether you show empathy to someone you pass in the street or to your most loved family member, it allows the other person to know that you've heard what's going on for them.

Secondly, it enables you to find mutually acceptable solutions, because when someone feels truly heard, their energy can shift into problem-solving mode with little effort. I love the description of empathy that Simon Baron-Cohen, Professor in the Departments of Psychology and Psychiatry at Cambridge University, gives: 'Empathy is like a universal solvent. Any problem immersed in empathy becomes soluble.'[2] Considering the huge range and scope of the problems we face as human beings, it's not hard to imagine how transformational a greater focus on empathy could be.

What exactly is empathy?

Given that empathy is so fundamental to creating connection, let's be clear about what it is. There are many definitions, but the one I find most helpful from a Needs Understanding perspective is: 'my understanding of your experience and feelings, with full acceptance and without judgement.' More conversationally, I'd describe it as: 'getting you so you know you've been got'.

I'd like to invite you to imagine two islands. You're on one and someone else is on the other. When you empathise with that person you sail across to their island, leaving your own behind. As you step ashore, you notice that the climate is different, the vegetation unfamiliar, and the territory mysterious and unexplained. You become curious about what it's like in this strange land, and how you might start to explore it. You can, of course, return to the comfortable familiarity of your own island at any time, but while you're visiting, you put your

---

[2] Simon Baron-Cohen, *Zero Degrees of Empathy: A New Understanding of Cruelty and Kindness* (London, Penguin, 2012).

thoughts about home to one side and choose to focus on the new world the other person is showing you. This is what it feels like to experience empathy for someone else.

Because empathy is characterised by unconditional acceptance and warmth, it involves 'getting' another person's whole experience in a way that allows them to know that they've been fully received and understood. This means more than gaining an intellectual understanding, in which you imagine what it's like for them but stop short of engaging emotionally. Full empathy involves developing a felt sense of what it's like to walk in their shoes and see the world through their eyes, as if you were them. Just for the time that you're visiting their island.

How can we learn to be more empathic?

For years, I was convinced I couldn't 'do empathy'. This self-defeating belief bothered me because I longed to be someone who was strong at relationships. Ironically, my concern about my lack of empathy got in the way of me becoming more empathic, because the more caught up I was in my own insecurities as I listened to other people, the less present I was to what they were saying. Today, I still smile inwardly whenever someone tells me what a good listener I am, because the reality used to be so different.

Empathy is a learnable skill that can change how we relate to people in a significant way. It also allows us to find routes through problems that work for everyone, with the potential to make our own lives – and the world around us – a better place.

There's no one set way to cultivate empathy, but if you're unsure about where to start you might find it helpful to break it down into two areas:

- **How to be:** developing an empathic attitude; and
- **What to say:** finding your authentic empathy language.

How to be: develop an empathic attitude

The foundation to becoming more empathic starts with having a compassionate approach towards yourself and other people. When you practise putting on your needs glasses to see that everything anyone says or does is an attempt to meet their needs, this can encourage you to tune in to what they really want underneath. Whenever you come across a situation in which you want to develop a deeper connection with someone, you can:

1. check you're in a good emotional space to listen;

2. give your full attention; and

3. choose a compassionate perspective.

1. Check you're in a good emotional space to listen

If you're exhausted at the end of a long day, have just come off a phone call in which someone gave you bad news, or life has thrown you a curve ball, you may need to give yourself time to recover before you can be available to someone else. Suppose you have an ongoing disagreement with your partner about them coming home late from work, leaving you to cook dinner alone each night; you're probably not in the right frame of mind to have a constructive conversation about it the minute they walk through the door. When you're focused on your own thinking, as you almost certainly are when you feel stressed, frustrated, or angry, you're unlikely to be able to truly hear what anyone says. This applies equally to those times when you feel judgemental about yourself: 'I'm not a good listener'; 'I've got it wrong again'; 'Why am I always like this?'

We'll look at how to deal with blaming thoughts about yourself or others in the next part of the book. For now, consider practising empathy in non-challenging scenarios. You could try crossing over to someone's island when they're telling you about something that they're happy about, or when it's a person you love being around. Make a mental note when you feel the impulse to jump in with advice or opinions, and experiment with keeping quiet instead.

This is important, because it's often the occasions when we most want to change our way of listening that are the ones where it's most difficult to do so. We may long to transform aspects of our relationships with our partners, parents, children, or that colleague who really gets to us. All of this is absolutely doable, but until we're comfortable with empathising in easy scenarios and have the tools to cope with our own reactivity, it's too big a challenge for many of us. Being in a good place for empathising means not being too caught up in our own stuff.

2. Give your full attention

For most of us, this is harder than it sounds. There are practical steps you can take to make it easier to listen, such as turning off your phone or making sure you won't be interrupted, but even then you'll probably notice that your mind has a life of its own. You may spot any number of mental distractions, such as your opinions about what the other person is saying or what you're going to have for dinner that night. It's as if your visit to their island is being disrupted by worrying storm clouds on the horizon, and all you can think of is how you're going to get home again.

When you notice your thoughts wandering off, you can choose to take it as a positive sign because it means that you're aware of it happening and can do something about it. Why not gently park them to one side with a promise to return later, and go back to the speaker's territory? In my experience, we continue to have wandering thoughts no matter how much practice with listening and empathy we have. Progress isn't about getting rid of them, but about learning to hold them to one side without judging ourselves, so we can keep our focus on the other person.

3. Choose a compassionate perspective

When you put on your needs glasses, you can see that everything the other person says and does is an attempt to meet their underlying needs. A helpful approach can be to ask yourself what they're longing for. What's important to them? What lies behind the words they're using? When you're in the realm of needs, you don't need to agree with their ideas or actions. You're just trying to get a real sense of this island that's their home.

Sometimes as you're listening, you may find yourself taking things personally, or notice you're judging the person you're with: 'Why on earth did he do that?' or 'You should have known that would happen.' This in turn might trigger thoughts about yourself: 'I've done it again – I should know how to listen by now,' or 'I'm such a rubbish friend!' If you find yourself consumed by defensiveness, justifications, or judgements, you're not able to be empathic. This is the same if you're holding on to an agenda for the other person to change their views. We'll explore how to transform these judgements in the next part of the book, but for now consider trying to put those thoughts to one side as best you can.

PAUSE BOX

Discover the 'yes' behind someone's 'no'

An interesting way of practising empathic listening is to ask yourself what the 'yes' behind someone's 'no' might be. In other words, when a person says 'no' to something that you've suggested, what are the needs that they're saying 'yes' to? What needs are they prioritising?

For instance, looking back on my story about my daughter when she refused to go to the café, the 'no' was to a trip out, while the 'yes' behind her 'no' was to her needs for fun and choice. When a colleague says 'no' to helping you on a piece of work, she may be saying 'yes' to her need for stimulation and interest, or perhaps for space and rest. Guessing what someone is saying 'yes' to can help you to explore solutions that will work for both you and them. In this sense, 'no' is just the start of a conversation.

You might like to try this retrospectively on a couple of your recent interactions. What needs might have been underneath the 'no' that you heard from another person?

Does guessing the needs at play mean that you experience the 'no' any differently now?

What to say: find your authentic empathy language

You've travelled to someone's island and are having a good look around, but what tools do you need to help you explore – a torch, a shovel, a pair of binoculars perhaps? When you're empathising, your words are your instruments. However, it can be hard to find the right ones to use. You may find it helpful to have suggested phrases to try out so that you can experiment with finding language that feels authentic to you. You may even find, in a 'fake it until you make it' approach, that the words help you to develop a more empathic attitude in their own right.

Alternatively, it's possible that you'll feel constrained by my suggested words and phrases, in which case feel free to ignore them. If you have an empathic attitude, any words have the potential to work. Equally, you can say all the 'right' words you like, but if your language doesn't reflect your internal reality it's unlikely to be heard as empathic.

If you'd enjoy some suggestions, here are five to play with:

- silence
- prompts
- summarising
- validation of feelings
- guessing feelings or needs

Silence

Empathy is all about the quality of the presence that we bring to the person speaking, and this doesn't necessarily need words. That presence can transmit itself just as powerfully through our silence, eye contact, and body language, as through our voice. If you're like me and naturally use a lot of words, or if you tend to over-think what to say, silence can be a very helpful option for standing alongside the other person.

Silence can also be a simple way to learn empathy skills, because with your mouth closed you don't need to think about what to say, and can practise being present. You can try it in meetings or conversations, keeping your curiosity focused on the person speaking, and – before responding – asking them if there's anything else they'd like to say.

Prompts

When you prompt someone, you're helping them to feel confident as they tell their story. It's one way of letting them know that you're following them and are interested in hearing more. Similar to the difference between clarifying and fact-finding that we explored when we looked at habitual listening, you're tuning into what you think they would most like to say, rather than taking the conversation off in the direction that you want to follow.

Here are some examples of open prompts you could use.

'What happened next?'

'How was that for you?'

'Is there more you'd like to tell me?'

'Mmmm…'

Summarising

Summarising or reflecting is when you try to capture the essence of what the other person has said, and reflect it back to them as a whole. You don't have to stick to the words they've used – you can summarise what seems important to them.

Here are some sentence starters you can use for summarising.

'I'm hearing that…'

'It sounds like…'

'What you're saying is…?'

'I'm understanding… Is that it?'

Validation of feelings

This is a powerful way for you to show that you're listening to the person speaking, because it involves recognising their feelings and acknowledging them as important. Validating doesn't mean that you agree with their perspective or approve of their choices, only that you understand them. Here are examples of how it could work.

'I can see why you'd be worried about that, given your previous experience.'

'Knowing what I do of the situation, I can well imagine...'

'It makes total sense that you'd feel angry when he said that.'

Guessing feelings or needs

Maintaining a compassionate presence involves connecting with the feelings and needs of the other person. When you notice these, you can voice them out loud with guesses.

'So you just want to be able to understand more in meetings?' (guessing a need for understanding)

'You're wanting to know you're a really valuable member of the team even if you aren't a manager?' (guessing a need for appreciation or recognition)

'Did you feel frustrated because no one listened to you?' (guessing a feeling of frustration and a need to be heard)

'I'm guessing you're delighted with the progress?' (guessing a feeling of excitement)

When you guess feelings and needs, you're not doing it to find the 'right' answer – in fact, it doesn't matter at all whether or not you guess correctly. What's important is that by guessing you move the conversation into the realm of the feelings and needs that are likely to bring mutual understanding and connection. And if you've guessed a need that doesn't fit, the other person can put you right, which gives them a stepping stone to talk about what's really going on for them.

Guessing does come with a bit of a warning, which is that it can lead you to live in your head while you intellectualise about what the speaker is feeling and needing. Separating yourself from your own feelings is not a good way to build connection. Your aim here is to sense empathically where the other person is coming from, and to stay present with it, so if you find guessing to be a distraction it may be an idea to try something else.

From empathy to action

As listeners, it also helps to spot when empathy has run its course in a conversation. You may find yourself recognising signs that flag up when the person speaking has received enough empathy for them to trust that they've been heard: they stop talking, give a sigh, or there's a shift in tone. You might also see some physical relief, such as their shoulders dropping or their face relaxing.

If there's a need for action to be taken, it's at this point that they'll often move seamlessly into finding a way forward. It's noticeable how the energy of this type of solution-finding is completely different from how it would have been if you hadn't offered them empathy. When we humans don't feel heard, we can get panicky and desperate, but when we feel secure in someone's empathy we find it easier to approach a problem with spaciousness and creativity. This is the moment when you can ask yourself: 'How can I be of most service here? What's the thing that will create the most connection? How can I best contribute to this person?' Any solutions they find, or that you come up with together, are likely to stick.

When I started designing online courses, I joined a mentoring group. During one of our sessions, a woman called Radhika arrived on the call seeming distracted and shaken. This was unusual for Radhika, who normally came across as organised and powerful. She told the group that she was struggling with a course launch, and we willingly pitched in with practical tips and advice. She diligently wrote everything down, but I wondered if she was taking anything in, and my sense grew that before she could even think about acting on this advice she might appreciate some empathy.

'Radhika,' I said. 'I'm noticing that you don't seem quite yourself today. I wonder if you'd like to say anything before we carry on?' At that moment she burst into tears – it was clear that what really mattered went way beneath the surface concerns about her launch. Later she sent me an email to say she felt much better, and was then able to put the tips into practice.

Some questions you may have about empathy

Can I use empathy with someone who's angry with me?

The short answer is yes – and, for most of us, it's one of the hardest times to empathise. Maybe the other person is upset at something you've done, or perhaps someone else has riled them and they're taking it out on you. Although these situations are difficult, they're also the ones in which showing empathy can be most powerful; people are unused to the person they're angry with being interested in their needs.

Given that this is so tricky, I suggest that you consider practising empathy in less charged scenarios at first. I only mention this type of conversation here in case it helps you to know from the outset that it is possible to be able to hear someone's anger without taking it personally (and without giving up on your own position), while at the same time looking for constructive ways forward. When we can empathise with someone who hates what we stand for, we shift the world another tiny step away from polarisation and towards closer understanding and cooperation.

What's the difference between empathy and sympathy?

We touched on this earlier, and I want to explore it again here because the distinction matters when we're getting to grips with how to empathise. In sympathy, I step into your shoes as me, and use my intellectual abilities to imagine your situation from my own perspective. In empathy, I also step into your shoes, but this time I try to see the situation from *your* perspective by using my feelings as well as my thoughts. It's as if I sense what it's like to be you right now, given who you are and what your experience is, rather than imagining how I would feel in your place.

Isn't empathy just a tactic for getting what I want?

Not if it's real empathy. Often, so-called empathy is used as a way to try to change someone's mind: 'I know what you mean, but…' or 'I see where you're coming from, but…'. With this, you're using something that looks like empathy to soften up the other person so that they're ready to accept your point of view.

The intention you have when you empathise is crucial. When you use it to try to get what you want, the other person is likely to sense what you're doing and to dig in their heels. Real empathy is all about understanding where someone else is coming from. It can result in a connection that makes a shift in perspective possible, because if they trust that you've 'got' their needs and are holding them with care, they're more likely to be open to listening to your different viewpoint. Even if they're not, you've still looked after your relationship by genuinely trying to understand their perspective, rather than pushing your own preferred solution.

How do I stop being overwhelmed by other people's feelings?

If you're the person all your colleagues come to for advice, leaving you exhausted by their problems, or you're the one who always tries to help people in your family and ends up feeling overwhelmed, it may be that you've drifted from empathy into the realm of over-giving.

Empathy is when you want to connect with someone by sensing their experience – by visiting their island – but only for as long as it works for *you* as well as for them. It's different from emigrating there and memorising the language and customs before you allow yourself to return home. If you over-identify with another person's feelings and take them on as your own, leaving you drained and incapable of managing your own concerns, that's over-giving. As we progress, we'll look more at how to recognise when to take care of your own needs, and how to set firm boundaries.

Can I do empathy my own way?

Of course! You can do what works for the two of you – using words (or not), keeping silent (or not), and doing something (or just staying by their side). A lovely example of this came from my friend Jamal, who was listening to his girlfriend Emma talk about all the reasons she was convinced she was going to fail with her new business. He started off by giving her advice and reassuring her that she'd be fine, which he soon realised was unhelpful – all he was doing was trying to 'fix' her. So he went away and came back a second time with a metaphor. He likened her new venture to the process of giving birth, and all that goes with it, so as to have a baby. It would be painful and messy for a while, but worth it in the end. This way of speaking wasn't his natural territory, but he was willing to cross over to Emma's island so he could make a connection with her. She appreciated it because the analogy was similar to the way she would have expressed her thoughts. This, together with the effort she could see he was making, made all the difference to how heard she felt.

If you only take one thing from this chapter…

- Listening with empathy is something that you can learn to do.

And if you take a few more…

- Empathic listening involves engaging with people's feelings in a way that works for them as well as for you.

- Knowing that whatever anyone says or does is an attempt to meet their needs gives you the basis for empathic listening.

- When you listen, you can use whatever language is authentic to express your understanding of the other person's experience.

- When a speaker knows that they've been empathised with, they're more likely to move towards their own creative solutions.

Understand yourself with COMPASSION

Part Two

Here we turn our attention towards our own needs. We can go through life unaware of our needs, not realising how they influence our thoughts and actions. When we become more aware of them, we're in a stronger position to take care of them. We can also see when we respond to them in unhelpful ways and what to do about it.

Chapter 4

What makes you tick? Getting to know your own needs

- How to connect with your needs
- Two guides to your needs
  - Guide one: the weather (your feelings)
  - Guide two: mythical monsters (your judgemental thoughts)
- Using the two guides to sense your needs
- When you've found, and felt, your needs

Chapter 5

How to unlock difficult situations: extra tools for tricky self-empathy

- Filling your internal tank
- When you're triggered by someone or something
- When you regret the way you've behaved

Chapter 4

What makes you tick?

Getting to know your own needs

You find yourself shouting at your children; you complain about your boss being overbearing and unreasonable; you tell yourself that you're no good at your job; you feel grumpy, anxious, or exhausted. Each of us has our own challenges in life, and seeing them through the lens of needs can help. The actions we don't like, the feelings we'd rather not feel, the judgemental thoughts about ourselves and others – in every situation we're just trying to meet our needs. But the problem is that we're sometimes doing it in a way that isn't working for us or for anyone else.

Let's remind ourselves of the two core principles of Needs Understanding.

- Principle 1: Our behaviour is always an attempt to meet our needs.

- Principle 2: Our world works best when our chosen strategies take care of everyone's needs.

Listening with empathy to someone, and discovering some of their needs, can be powerful. But what about your own needs? How do you find out what they are? And how can they help you? In this part of the book we'll explore how to apply the principles of Needs Understanding to ourselves, in an empathic way.

Paying attention to our own needs can feel uncomfortable or strange at first. We may not be used to exploring our inner world, or we may believe that doing so is self-indulgent. We might not think much about our needs, and if we do see a need, we may assume that it's not reasonable or even possible to meet it. Sometimes we can feel overwhelmed by our needs and unsure what to do about them. Needs Understanding offers a way of finding and meeting our own needs so that we can live our lives more fully and contribute effectively in the wider world.

The purpose of this chapter is to give you ways of discovering your needs. Knowing your own needs can help you to deal with difficult feelings, communicate more effectively, be there more fully for other people, and find ways out of problems that work for you and everyone else. In the following chapter, we'll look at some additional pointers for applying this understanding in particularly challenging situations.

How to connect with your needs

Previously, I likened listening to someone with empathy to sailing from your island to theirs and having a look around. Now I'm inviting you to explore your own island. You may notice that your needs run across it like crystal clear streams of water. They bubble and wander, nurturing the earth and giving life to everything around them.

When you're curious about what's making you behave as you do, you can ask yourself, 'What is it that I'm needing here?' Sometimes you may be able to spot the streams and identify what's going on for you straightaway. You might find that looking at the list of needs can help you. Often, though, it takes some practice to find your needs. They can be hidden deep in the forests of confusion or in the dark caves of the island that you'd rather not enter; they can even run underground, where you've yet to discover them.

Two guides to your needs

Luckily, your island is equipped with two knowledgeable guides, who are there to help. They remind you to pay attention to your needs, and they point you towards where to find them. These guides have different characteristics: one is the weather in all its forms, and it represents your feelings. The other is a group of mythical monsters, who represent your judgemental thoughts. They might seem unlikely allies, but you can make use of them to explore all sorts of difficult situations.

Before we go any further, let's remember that our needs are often trickiest to find in the middle of highly charged situations. You may like first to use the guides out of the heat of the moment. Then, as you become more practised at connecting with your needs and learn which show up for you at different times, your guides can become part of your natural thinking process.

Guide one: the weather (your feelings)

Your first guide is the weather – in other words, your varying feelings. It could be a gentle breeze, the roaring heat, or a freezing downpour; like your feelings, the weather can take any number of guises and can change in a moment.

If I were to say to you, 'What are you feeling right now?' you may or may not be able to tell me. We're all different in how easy we find it to experience and describe our feelings. Some of us had upbringings in which we learned how to express and regulate our feelings; others of us did not. We may have been repeatedly told that 'anger isn't nice', or 'there's no need to be upset', which taught us that some feelings weren't welcome. Or we may have lived in families in which big feelings like grief and rage were expressed in frightening ways, so that we felt unsafe. The outcome of this as adults can be that we're unsure how to manage our own feelings. We may stifle some of them and find ourselves overcome by others. We may feel numb and out of touch with what's going on inside.

However, when we learn to pay attention to our feelings, we can understand them as a direct indicator of our underlying needs. Feelings such as happiness, satisfaction, and joy generally signal that our needs are being met, while feelings like anger, sadness, or anxiety tell us that our needs are not being met.

For instance, you might notice that you feel unhappy. What need could lie behind the unhappiness? It might be that you have a need for intimacy that's not being satisfied at the moment. Or perhaps it's more like connection? Or companionship? On the other hand, let's say that you're feeling delighted at the prospect of heading out for a picnic. What's the need there that's being met? Is it rejuvenation? Pleasure? Fun? I only use these connections between feelings and needs as examples, because these specific feelings could link to any number of needs, depending on who you are and what circumstance you're in.

Here's a list of feelings to help you to pinpoint what might be going on for you at any given moment. You'll also find it at the end of the book for reference.

LIST OF FEELINGS

Glad, happy, hopeful, joyful, satisfied, delighted, blissful, courageous, grateful, confident, relieved, touched, proud, optimistic, overjoyed, warm, wonderful.

Excited, amazed, amused, exuberant, astonished, breathless, eager, energetic, enthusiastic, fascinated, inspired, interested, intrigued, stimulated.

Peaceful, calm, content, expansive, blissful, satisfied, relaxed, secure, clear, comfortable, pleasant, relieved.

Loving, warm, affectionate, tender, friendly, sensitive, compassionate, nurtured, trusting, helpful, moved.

Playful, energetic, refreshed, alert, stimulated, exuberant, adventurous, eager, enthusiastic, curious.

Rested, relaxed, alert, refreshed, strong, alive, energised.

Thankful, grateful, appreciative, fulfilled.

Sad, lonely, heavy, helpless, grieving, overwhelmed, distant, discouraged, distressed, dismayed, concerned, depressed, despairing, disappointed.

Yearning, longing, nostalgic, remorseful, pining, aching, regretful, wistful.

Scared, afraid, fearful, terrified, nervous, panicky, horrified, anxious, lonely, sceptical, suspicious, alarmed, apprehensive, frightened, jealous, surprised.

Angry, aggravated, frustrated, furious, mad, enraged, hostile, pessimistic, resentful, disgusted, annoyed, disappointed, displeased, upset.

Confused, hesitant, troubled, torn, uneasy, worried, apprehensive, bewildered, disturbed, reluctant, insecure.

Tired, exhausted, indifferent, overwhelmed, burnt out, helpless, heavy, sleepy, withdrawn, apathetic, bored, lazy, numb.

Uncomfortable, pained, uneasy, hurt, miserable, embarrassed, ashamed, guilty, impatient, irritated, restless.

If you tend to find it hard to identify your feelings, even if it's only at particular moments, you may find that it helps to focus on what's going on in your body. When something happens in our internal or external environment, we react physically, and we use the language of feelings to interpret those reactions. For instance, if you notice that you're hunched up and tense, it may tell you that you're feeling stressed or worried. If you experience warmth, or a sense of relaxation and openness, you may say that you feel happy. Many of us are so used to living in our heads that we forget to call on our bodily resources, but becoming aware of physical sensations can be a way of connecting with our feelings. There's a list of physical sensations at the end of the book, which you can use to help identify what's going on for you.

PAUSE BOX

Practise linking your feelings to your needs

Have to hand: the list of needs.

This is a needs body scan that gives you some practice in linking your feelings to your needs. You may want to close your eyes as you engage with each step. If you find yourself becoming distracted, gently bring your attention back to your breathing and body.

1. Make yourself comfortable and take a few deep breaths, noticing the feeling of your breath coming in and out of your body.

2. Focus on your head. What physical sensations do you notice? It could be warmth, tension, thudding, tightness, or something else.

3. Move slowly through the different parts of your body, from your head to your toes. Just as with your head, notice the physical sensations in each.

4. When you've been through your whole body ask yourself: 'Are there any words that describe how I feel? Am I anxious? Tired? Contented? Irritable? Something else?'

5. Take a look at your list of needs. Ask yourself what needs might be behind how you feel. If you're anxious, are you wanting to know that you're 'enough' just as you are? If you're happy, is it because you're loving a close connection in a relationship today?

6. Reflect on what you've discovered, and on how you may want to apply it going forward.

You could also reflect on what might be behind particularly strong feelings when they arise. Remember when we looked at the list of needs right at the beginning, and explored how certain needs can crop up for us again and again? These are fingerprint needs, and they arouse big feelings. The characteristics that distinguish them from our other needs are that they come up repeatedly, and that they provoke powerful reactions in us when they do. If we aren't aware of our fingerprint needs we may not understand why we're reacting the way we are, but we can use our feelings to guide us towards these needs if we know what to look out for. We'll consider this more fully later on; meanwhile, when you next find yourself reacting strongly to someone or something, you may want to ask yourself if one of your fingerprint needs is involved. And if you aren't yet sure what your fingerprint needs are, reflecting on these strong reactions is one way to discover them.

Our emotional life is an essential part of how we relate to ourselves and those around us. If we can start to understand that our feelings are valuable messengers about our needs, we can accept them, make sense of what they're telling us, and act on them with awareness. Rightly understood, our feelings are a resource rather than a distraction that gets in the way. They're an indicator of what's important to us in any given moment.

Guide two: mythical monsters (your judgemental thoughts)

Alongside your feelings you have a second – perhaps unexpected – set of guides to your needs, especially when things aren't flowing easily for you. These are your judgemental thoughts. I like to think of them as mythical monsters that hide in the forests and caves of your island. They have spikes running down their backs, piercing eyes, and green, scaly bodies; they spend most of their time grumbling quietly to themselves, but are capable of the most hideous roar when provoked.

What do I mean by these monsters, or rather, our judgemental thoughts about ourselves, others, or a situation? We can think about them as being split into different groups.

- **Finding fault and blaming:** it's my fault; you make me feel so angry; if she'd only…

- **Evaluating and labelling:** I'm a bad parent; she's so difficult; it's outrageous behaviour; this government is stupid.

- **Shoulds and oughts:** I should know better; I ought to have done that by now; you should have thought of it beforehand.

- **Comparing:** she's much better at it than me; why can't you be more like him?

- **Demands and threats:** you have to do this; if you don't do it, I'll…

- **Black and white thinking:** I always make the same mistake; you talk about it but you never change anything.

- **Moralising:** rushing your work is wrong; liberal thinking is right; dropping litter is bad; paying tax is good.

We may not want to admit to these thoughts, even though most of us have hundreds of them each and every day. Some of us are inclined to unleash our judgemental thoughts onto other people by arguing with them. Others of us have a tendency to be harsh with ourselves instead, feeling shame and guilt when we do. Often we swing between the two: angry thoughts towards someone or something else, and then guilt for thinking that way.

Judgemental thoughts aren't pretty, and are often accompanied by difficult feelings such as anger, guilt, shame, numbness, depression, or anxiety. Because of this we're in the habit of justifying them, ignoring them, feeling ashamed of them, or pretending that they aren't there. Like mythical monsters, it's natural to find them frightening and ugly at first and to want to run away from them, but these monsters are hungry for attention. If we don't pay them enough, they only roar more loudly. And here's the thing: although they seem unfriendly, if we can summon the courage to approach them with compassion, they'll repay us by sharing the treasures they keep hidden. These treasures are our needs.

So I want to encourage you – counter-intuitive as it may seem – to welcome your judgemental thoughts with as much empathy, warmth, and even celebration as you can muster. That's because once we can spot the monsters, listen to them, and start to find the important unmet needs behind them, we can take care of our needs in ways which are less likely to hurt ourselves or others. The more we see and understand them, the less our monsters have to growl at us to attract our attention, and the better we can hear what they're trying to tell us about ourselves. We'll gradually start feeling angry and guilty less often, and stop behaving in ways that we don't like.

Until recently, my daughter would, despite constant reminders, find something that needed to be done for school at the last minute each Sunday evening. I would immediately jump to having judgemental thoughts about her: 'We go through this every week! How come you haven't learned by now? This is so unfair on me. You've ruined the end of the weekend yet again! It's all your fault.' I would then swing quickly into guilt, saying to myself: 'I'm such a harsh mother. She's so good at remembering most things, and this is completely normal behaviour for her age. If only I were more patient and understanding.'

Once I'd spotted the weekly pattern, I turned to listen to my judgemental thoughts. In this case, it was easy to find my needs behind them – for ease, relaxation, and connection with my daughter, together with my longing to contribute to her with love and warmth. Realising this, I resolved to talk to her at a relaxed moment rather than mid-crisis, and it was fairly straightforward to find strategies together to break the cycle of last-minute panics.

PAUSE BOX

Welcome the monsters: discover the needs behind your judgemental thoughts

Have to hand: the list of needs, and a pen and paper.

Take a look at the types of judgemental thoughts above, and use them to prompt you to think of one that you're having about yourself or someone else.

Make a note of the thought, and of how you're feeling right now.

Now turn to the list of needs. With the thought in mind, ask yourself: 'What need(s) do I have here?'

Note down any needs that feel like they could fit.

How do you feel now? If you've sensed some needs that match well, you may notice a physical shift in your body as you recognise what's really behind your initial judgemental thought.

Judgemental thoughts can be an indication of all kinds of needs, including fingerprint needs. A friend told me that he'd spent much of his life with the assumption that earning a lot of money was a sign of high worth. Plenty of people had told him why it didn't make sense to think like that, but it was a hard notion for him to shake. However, he started to explore this belief through the lens of needs.

He realised that he was having judgemental thoughts about how he 'should' be living his life. He noticed that they were linked to a fingerprint need from childhood, when he didn't experience feeling valued for who he was, but for what he achieved. As an adult, he veered between trying to suppress his belief by rebelling against 'the system' and earning very little, and submitting to it by working long hours to fill up his bank account. Neither approach gave him the feeling of being worthwhile that he longed for. Now he's starting to take responsibility for finding his own sense of value separately from his salary, and at the same time to look for work that reflects his inner purpose but that still pays him enough to live the life he wants.

Using the two guides to sense your needs

Now that you're familiar with how feelings and judgemental thoughts can point you towards your needs, it's time to put them together. Here's the relationship between needs, feelings and judgemental thoughts:

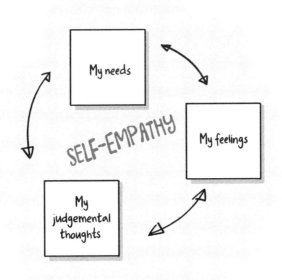

Moving between feelings, judgemental thoughts, and needs isn't a linear process – you can transition between all three of them in any direction, and as often as you like, as you explore your needs. Your aim is to do this until you've reached the point of sensing what's going on for you.

I'd also love you to notice the comforting cushion of self-empathy that surrounds this process. In the last chapter we defined empathy as 'my understanding of your experience and feelings, with full acceptance and without judgement'. We can define self-empathy in the same way but in relation to ourselves: 'my understanding of my own experience and feelings, with full acceptance and without judgement.'

Self-empathy is important, because discovering your needs means that you need to be ready to face difficult feelings and thoughts. When you mess up, self-empathy helps you to move beyond guilt so that you can discover your needs and make constructive changes going forward. When you have uncomfortable feelings, it encourages you to allow yourself to feel them so that you can use them as a guide. You can ask yourself, 'How are you feeling? It's okay to feel that way. It's normal to be angry sometimes. What do you need right now?'

Using your feelings and judgemental thoughts as guides to your needs is one of those ideas that might be hard to grasp without having a go at putting it into practice, so if you only do one Pause Box, this might be the one.

PAUSE BOX

Uncover your needs in a current situation

Have to hand: three sheets of paper and a pen.

Recall a recent interaction that you didn't enjoy. Maybe you felt angry or upset; maybe you argued with someone; maybe you managed a meeting poorly; maybe you found yourself talking to your child in a way that you vowed you never would.

Put on your needs glasses to remind yourself that whatever happened, you (and everyone else) were only trying to meet the needs at play. As you do the following exercise, aim to explore those needs with the same empathy, warmth, and acceptance for yourself that you learned to practise with others.

Take three sheets of paper and write down a heading on each: Feelings, Judgemental Thoughts, Needs.

Now take a few moments to think and feel yourself back into the situation as best you can. Notice any feelings, and jot them down on the relevant sheet. Do the same with judgemental thoughts and needs, remembering that you can jump around from one sheet to another. You may find that you write down some judgemental thoughts, then connect them with feelings, and then connect them with more judgemental thoughts, followed by a need – and so on.

When you're sensing what needs may be involved, keep a particular eye out for any needs that you may already have identified as your fingerprint needs.

If you prefer, you can place the sheets on the floor and walk to each one, instead of writing on them.

How do you feel now? Does uncovering your needs give you any fresh insights?

Let's look at an example of using your thoughts and feelings to connect with your needs. Imagine you're giving a presentation to ten senior people at work, with the aim of persuading them to agree to a budget increase for your project. You've spent hours preparing and practising it beforehand, and when the big day comes you walk to the front of the room with a dry mouth and racing heart. You launch into the talk, and initially sense that the audience is paying attention. Then halfway through, you notice that one of the managers is looking at her phone, and another one is stifling a yawn. This knocks you off your stride, and the second half is scrappier than you would have liked. As you end the presentation, you have a sinking feeling that it could have gone better.

Given that you often need to give presentations, you're keen to reflect on how to do it differently next time. So you give it some thought later that evening when you've eaten a meal and have the mental space to think clearly. What kind of judgemental thoughts do you notice as you put yourself back into the room? 'What a cheek, scrolling through her phone. How rude was that?' (judging the other person). And, 'I must be the most boring presenter in the world if people are falling asleep in the middle of my talk' (judging yourself).

What about your feelings? As you relive the situation, you feel a memory of the wave of shock when you noticed people not paying attention, together with a tightness in your chest and hotness in your cheeks. While you have some embarrassment, your main feeling is anger.

And what about your needs? Running down the list of needs, you remember the sense of being ignored, and quickly realise that the standout one for you is recognition. You want to be seen for the value of your project. As you connect with your need, you experience a shift away from anger and towards sadness and relief.

A couple of insights follow. Firstly, you remember how the need for recognition has played out like a theme tune in your life – there during your schooldays when you didn't see your name on the noticeboard lists, there as a young adult when looking for praise from your managers at work, and still present now in this example. Recognition is a fingerprint need for you, and each time you see it for what it is (along with a healthy dose of self-empathy), you're less likely to be ambushed by it, and more likely to find healthy ways to meet it. In this case, you might have asked supportive colleagues for feedback at the end of the presentation, starting with someone who you know was appreciative of the work you've done.

Secondly, you think of the two managers involved. 'She was only glancing at her phone – maybe she was waiting for an important message. And the other guy was probably just tired. But no wonder I took it to heart, given that my fingerprint need was being touched on. I don't need to beat myself up for getting it out of proportion. And next time, I'm less likely to be thrown off course by my need for recognition overtaking me without me realising.'

When you've found, and felt, your needs

Once you've unearthed your needs, much can shift. You may feel differently about the situation or relationship in question when you have a new perspective. It's hard to describe exactly how it works because you really need to experience it for yourself, but when you know what it is that you need, you can gain a new sense of clarity and empowerment.

Self-empathy can sometimes be enough on its own for you to move forward with whatever is troubling you. After all, self-compassion and understanding help you to recognise and accept your thoughts and feelings as being natural attempts to meet your needs. Once you've experienced this, solutions can often present themselves effortlessly.

You can also seek empathy from other people – and it doesn't have to be from someone who knows about Needs Understanding. What you're looking for is a person who can provide a warm, non-judgemental presence, and who's willing to listen while you get things off your chest. Alternatively you can do deeper work, either alone or with others – this can be particularly helpful with your fingerprint needs, which need special love and care. Meditation, journaling, bodywork, visualisation, psychotherapy, inner child work, and religious practice are examples of disciplines that can offer you the experience of having your unmet needs met.

Welcoming your feelings and judgemental thoughts means noticing them and making the most of the messages they have to give you. That doesn't mean that you have to like them or want them to stay around – often quite the reverse. However, by acknowledging your thoughts and feelings, their energy has less of a grip on you. When you connect with the needs that they're pointing to, you become freer to live in the way you want, because you're not unconsciously trying to meet your needs at a cost to yourself and those around you.

If you only take one thing from this chapter…

- Getting to know your needs means that you can take care of them in a way that works for yourself and others.

And if you take a few more…

- Understanding yourself with compassion means recognising that your actions are understandable attempts to meet your needs.

- When you experience difficult feelings, or have judgemental thoughts, receiving yourself with warmth and empathy can be a first step towards change.

- You can welcome your feelings and judgemental thoughts as indicators of your underlying needs.

- Reflecting on difficult situations can help you to identify your fingerprint needs.

Chapter 5

How to unlock difficult situations

Extra tools for tricky self-empathy

In the last chapter, we looked at how to explore what's going on for us by using our feelings and judgemental thoughts as guides. We saw how they can help us to connect with our needs, find empathy for ourselves, and create new possibilities for ways forward.

You may have started to try out these skills in situations you face in your life. In my experience there are two types of recurring scenario that many of us find especially hard to deal with, and where I'd like to offer some additional pointers for understanding ourselves with compassion. They are:

- when you're triggered by someone or something; and
- when you regret the way that you've behaved.

Triggering

This term is used by different people in different ways. When I use it, I mean when something happens and you're caught in a surge of overpowering feelings that seem completely out of proportion to it. For instance, you panic when you're unexpectedly put on the spot; you're filled with murderous rage when your child hits their sibling; or you feel a cold wash of shame when you're caught doing something you think you shouldn't be. Along with experiencing very strong feelings, you're likely to react instantly in a way that you don't enjoy – perhaps you bluster, you yell, or you're struck speechless.

Regret

This is when you've behaved in ways that you wish you hadn't and find it almost impossible to deal with. Instead of knowing how to feel healthy regret, make amends, and find a guilt-free way forwards, you become stuck in guilty feelings about yourself.

Because these two types of situation tend to come up a lot and because they're so challenging, you're likely to be able to make a significant difference to your life if you can find ways of discovering the needs that are alive in them. Then even the most difficult of circumstances can feel easier to manage than you might imagine.

But first, let's have a look at what I call 'filling your internal tank'. This is always important, but is all the more so when you face your trickiest scenarios.

Filling your internal tank

Some days I sit at my desk in the morning and feel over-whelmed by all the tasks I have that day. 'I'll never manage all this,' I think, as my stomach tightens and my shoulders hunch. 'I can't get through it! I don't even know where to start.' The next day, however, I can look at exactly the same volume of work but without any stressful feelings at all. 'There's a lot on my to do list today,' I think. 'I'm looking forward to getting it all ticked off. Where shall I start?'

Why the difference? There could be a number of reasons, but often it's because in the first experience I feel depleted, and in the second I'm resourced. It's the same sort of feeling you may recognise if you're a parent. You walk in the door to be greeted by your child bombarding you with, 'Can I have this?' and 'Can I have that?' If you've just come back from coffee with a friend you may answer with a joke, or say, 'No, you can't have that now' but in an empathic way. If you've just had a day of stressful meetings, you might snap at your child to leave you alone, or give in and then feel annoyed or guilty.

When you resource yourself by proactively meeting your needs, it's a powerful way of increasing your productivity, effectiveness, and joy. When you leave it to chance and your internal tank runs dry, it's hard to look after your own or anyone else's needs. A full tank is a great tool for helping you to deal with whatever comes up, no matter how challenging it might be.

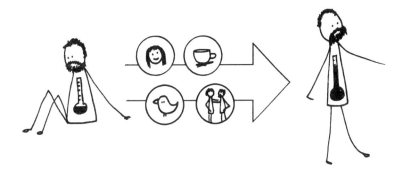

So how do you fill your tank? It may be helpful to ask yourself two questions:

1. 'What resources me?'

What brings you joy and a readiness to meet the world? It's different for everyone, and it might not be what you think *should* resource you. For me, going for a coffee in a café is infinitely more resourcing than a walk in the park, and a swim fills up my internal tank much more than an energetic cycle ride. There are no rights or wrongs – what's important is to find out what works best for you.

PAUSE BOX

Learn what fills your internal tank

Have to hand: a pen and paper.

For each of the following prompts, jot down a couple of activities that resource you:

- on your own;
- with others;
- outside;
- indoors;
- that cost money;
- that are free;
- that take a few minutes; and
- that take a few hours.

You may think of more. What matters is not the type of activity, but whether it leaves you feeling better able to deal with the world.

2. 'Do I resource myself enough, and if not, what stops me?'

Many of us aren't as well-resourced as we could be, and come up with reasons why we can't take the time to top up our tanks. You might recognise the following.

'It's selfish'

The idea that it's self-indulgent to look after our needs is a strong cultural, and sometimes religious, message that many of us have grown up with. Sometimes this can come from our upbringing. We might have had a caregiver who either ran themselves ragged putting everyone else first, or who made themselves a priority so that we felt as if our needs didn't matter. Or possibly one who flip-flopped between the two. Some of us were told directly that we should always put the needs of others before our own, while others absorbed the same message from watching how those around us behaved. These experiences can lead to us having a difficult relationship with the notion of taking care of ourselves.

Because the assumption that taking care of our needs is selfish runs so deep, it can be hard for us to see it for what it is – a way of thinking, rather than an objective truth. Another way of looking at it is to see that the better we take care of our needs, the better able we are to be available for other people. If you struggle with the idea of taking care of your needs, I invite you to try out this alternative viewpoint and see whether it fits for you.

'I don't have time' or 'I have more important things to do'

We tend to spend time on things that we've decided matter to us, so if you think you don't have time to spend on yourself, it might be that you don't see it as important enough. It could be that you feel it's selfish, as we explored above. Or it could just be a habitual way of thinking that you've slipped into. You might like to ask yourself, 'What tiny step could I take to create five minutes each day for me?'

When Aisha first came across Needs Understanding, she thought she was pretty adept at taking care of her emotional wellbeing. If she'd had a stressful day, her favourite way to unwind was with an episode or two of her favourite TV show. However, it was a huge insight to her when she realised that what she'd thought of as filling up her resource tank was, in fact, a partial denial of her needs. Retreating to the sofa met her need for comfort, but after a day of lone working she also had an unmet need for connection. Following this realisation, she started to reach for the phone rather than the TV remote when she came home, and to call her sister for a chat. This small habit change left her feeling resourced in a way that worked for her.

Now that we've explored the importance of filling up your internal tank, we'll move on to the two types of difficult situation in which an awareness of your needs can be transformational: when you're triggered, and when you regret the way you've behaved.

When you're triggered by someone or something

Dan had his mother to stay. They were having a cup of coffee when she asked, for the third time since breakfast, 'What will you be doing this weekend?' Dan felt burning anger rise within him. Blood rushed to his face, and he started to break into a sweat. Within a second of her question he snapped at her, 'I've told you a hundred times already what I'm doing! I know you find it difficult, but really, it's ridiculous that you ask me about every one of my movements!' Even in the moment, Dan was aware that he was caught up in a rush of emotion, but he couldn't stop himself reacting. Dan had been triggered.

As mentioned earlier, a trigger is when something happens and we're hit by a sudden, overwhelming feeling that seems disproportionate to what's going on. For Dan, instead of answering his mum briefly and then moving on to another subject, he had an automatic reaction that involved acting on his trigger before he'd even realised it was there.

How do you recognise when you're triggered? Typically you may:

- have a strong rush of emotion such as anger, panic, or shame;
- feel as if your emotions are in control of you, rather than the other way around;
- have judgemental thoughts about yourself or others;
- act in ways that you don't like, but can't seem to change;
- feel as you did when you were a child; or
- react automatically, rather than choosing a conscious response.

Trigger situations are a problem because they can get in the way of our relationships and sense of wellbeing. Let's look at what happens when we're triggered, and what we can do about it.

What's going on when we're triggered?

There's a saying: 'if it's hysterical, it's historical.' As we saw in the last chapter, feelings and judgemental thoughts are indicators of the needs that we might want to pay attention to. In trigger situations, the reason we react so strongly is that the needs that are touched upon are ones we have a particular history with. Most often, they're our fingerprint needs – the ones we experienced as not being met when we were children.

Back then, our caregivers not meeting our needs was a survival issue, and could, in the worst cases, have led to us being unable to live. As adults in trigger situations we aren't struggling for survival, but our brains don't make the distinction between then and now. We perceive unmet fingerprint needs as being a threat to our very existence, causing us to leap inappropriately into survival mode. The pre-frontal cortex part of our brain shuts down, making us incapable of rational thought, and our limbic brain – the seat of our emotions – takes over.

There are four survival responses when we're triggered: fight, flight, freeze, and (a less familiar one, perhaps) fawn. Which of these comes to the fore depends both on the situation and on our experiences of life.

- **Fight** is the aggression response: shouting, exerting control, slamming, raging.

- **Flight** is the avoidance response: panicking, withdrawing, avoiding, immersing ourselves in something else.

- **Freeze** is the rabbit-in-the-headlights response: becoming physically immobilised, being unable to make a decision, not knowing what to say, being unable to take a next step.

- **Fawn** is the people-pleasing response: accommodating, appeasing, flattering, agreeing, moulding ourselves around the other person.

When Dan's mum asked about his plans, Dan leapt into fight mode. His mum had unwittingly touched on his fingerprint needs for autonomy and agency. As a child, he had longed to be able to make choices about his life without anyone telling him off or getting in his way. Many years later, his mum is touching on those same needs with her questions, and he finds it impossible not to lash out at her.

What to do when you're triggered

Our reactions to situations that trigger us are often the ones that we're most desperate to change so that they don't keep disrupting our lives and relationships. These automatic responses are also some of the most stubborn habits to break because we're up against some powerful brain chemistry. That's why I'm breaking down the process of defusing triggers into two parts: what to do in the moment to stop yourself acting on a trigger, and what to do later, so you can learn to transform your triggers over time.

You experience a trigger:

In the moment: pause and rebalance

When you're caught up in a trigger, your aim is to interrupt the link between your automatic limbic system response – the rush of emotion you feel – and what you do next. You're trying to create a pause between the two. The larger you can make the gap, the more space there is for you to choose a conscious response rather than being caught up in an automatic reaction. You now have a wider set of choices available to you. In Dan's case, he can learn to recognise the signs that he's been triggered, such as the rush of blood to his face and the sweating he experiences. Then the challenge is to stop before he snaps at his mother – that's where he can, with practice, learn to pause and return to emotional equilibrium before he responds.

There are many ways to pause and rebalance. One of the most popular is to breathe deeply and slowly so that your body calms down physically. As you come back to a more grounded place, you may also find it helpful to remind yourself with empathy what's going on – that you're caught in a trigger because some deep, fingerprint needs have been touched on, and that it's hard to break the pattern.

pause and rebalance

Taking a physical break from the scene can also help. If you've been triggered by a person it's probably wise to stop talking, reminding yourself that you can always come back to the conversation later. You don't need to have the last word right then. In any case, it's likely that your point won't be fully heard when you express it mid-trigger.

If you're in fight mode and can't stop yourself from saying something, you can shout about your own needs rather than about what the other person has (or hasn't) done. 'Stop breathing down my neck!' becomes, 'I really need some space to think!', or 'Shut up!' becomes, 'I need peace and quiet!'

Whatever you do, it's probably not a great idea to try to come up with solutions to the problem there and then. Your 'thinking brain' simply isn't available to you in the middle of a trigger reaction – it's gone offline.

And finally, it's easy to underestimate how hard it is to break the link between trigger and reactive behaviour and to create a gap instead. Reminding ourselves what's going on within our brain chemistry can be helpful in finding the compassion and resilience we need to make changes.

Later: understand and learn from your trigger

After the situation has passed, take time to explore what was going on for you at the level of needs. If you do this often enough, you'll find that it helps to reduce both the strength and the frequency of your triggers. You may start to recognise what's going on in the heat of the moment, so that you can bring some understanding and empathy into the situation. This will enable you to make choices that are more likely to take care of your needs and those of the people around you.

When you look at triggers, it can be useful to connect with your past experiences. You may find you can remember times from your childhood when you felt similar to how you feel in a trigger situation. You might also find that the judgemental thoughts you have when you're triggered remind you of voices from the past. Keep a particular eye out for your fingerprint needs, because one or more of them is likely to have been alive for you at the time.

Eva and her partner were having a romantic wedding anniversary picnic. She'd spent a lot of time decorating a special cake and shopping for the food that they loved to share, and now they were sitting in a beautiful spot she'd found earlier in the day. It was going exactly as she'd hoped. Then she noticed a uniformed man approaching. 'Excuse me,' he said, 'but you can't sit here. This part of the park is closed to the public.'

Immediately, Eva felt a wave of shame. Her face flushed, she felt queasy, and all she could think about was how she wanted the ground to swallow her up. What was going on? It was only a park warden doing his job – there was no need to feel so awful.

Fast forward to the day after, and Eva was using Needs Understanding to explore her trigger reaction. Focusing first on her feelings, it was easy for her to reconnect with the sense of shame she'd felt. She noticed that it was as if she'd been transported back to being five years old and not able to tie her shoelaces in school. She was trying desperately to get it right, but ended up pretending she could do them, only for the teacher to spot her incompetence and pull her out of the line to do them up herself.

Eva reconnected with her judgemental thoughts, all of which turned inwards towards herself, rather than outwards at her partner or the warden: 'I've got it wrong'; 'I'm so stupid'; 'I should pay more attention'; 'I just wanted to have a lovely picnic and I've spoiled it all.' She could quickly pull out her need, which was something like, 'To be enough just as I am.'

Looking back on her childhood, she remembered always having a sense that she was trying hard but couldn't quite get it right, as in the shoelaces incident. When the picture of herself as a five-year-old girl floated before her eyes, she felt a wave of empathy and compassion for that child. She'd found a fingerprint need, one that she saw she'd need to take care of so as to build resilience to times when things don't work out. This would be the key to her doing what she wanted in the present without her past getting in the way.

PAUSE BOX

Understand your triggers

Have to hand: the list of needs, and a pen and paper.

Write down three headings on your paper: Judgemental Thoughts, Feelings, Needs.

1. Think of a recent situation in which you were triggered. Take yourself back to what went on in your body and mind.

2. As you notice judgemental thoughts or feelings, jot them down under the relevant headings.

3. Ask yourself: 'Does this remind me of any-thing from my childhood? Do the judgemental thoughts sound like anyone I know?'

4. Finally, if you haven't already, use the list of needs to identify which ones might have been alive for you in the situation. Can you spot any fingerprint needs among them?

As ever, when you practise self-compassion, you may find that it's enough simply to acknowledge that you have needs that weren't met in the triggering moment. That can give you an emotional shift, as it did for Eva. And just like when someone else truly hears and understands you, hearing and understanding yourself can also give you space for new insights and ways forward. Over time, as you become more practised with Needs Understanding, you'll learn to notice triggers more quickly, defuse them so they control you less, and draw on your self-empathy in the moment so that they're less likely to hurt you or those around you.

When you regret the way you've behaved

Whenever we behave in ways we don't like, we're attempting to meet our needs. If I shout at my child to be quiet, I'm longing for peace and calm. However, by shouting – even if I get those things – I don't meet my need for connection with her, or my need to contribute to her happiness and wellbeing. If we can make sense of the behaviour that we don't like in ourselves, we can more easily make amends and learn for next time, free from guilt.

Recently, I had what I'd imagined was going to be an exciting and productive conference call with three people from a client organisation. I'd been working with them for some time, we were all enjoying the collaboration, and we'd set up the half-hour meeting to discuss how to take our work to the next level. An agenda was agreed ahead of time, and all was set.

Things got off to a difficult start for me when one of the participants began the call with an account of a funding bid that she'd put in. It was unrelated to our agenda, and she spent the first half of our allotted time telling us all about it. I tried to move the conversation towards our purpose, but no one else seemed inclined to do the same, and I became more and more frustrated. However, instead of explaining what was going on for me so that we could agree how we wanted to use our remaining time, I became shorter and shorter with my answers in a way that made it clear how I felt, even though I didn't say so. We finished the call without talking about what mattered to me.

After we rang off, I began to feel guilty. 'I'm being selfish, only thinking of my own objectives. My colleague was excited, and I should have been glad about the funding bid news – how self-centred of me.' I felt full of regret for the way I'd behaved.

In a scenario like this it's usually not hard to identify our judgemental thoughts about ourselves. What can be more difficult is to bring in some self-empathy and understanding. So when you're feeling a sense of guilt, embarrassment, or shame, as I did coming off the call, I want to offer a tool that can help. It's called 'phone an imaginary friend', where our friend represents the inner compassion that's sometimes hard for us to find for ourselves.

Our friend reminds us that whatever we've done was only an attempt to meet our needs. 'It's understandable you feel bad. That call meant a lot to you, and it didn't go as well as you wanted. You were short and irritable because you were longing for partnership, and to set up a project with all sorts of exciting new possibilities. It matters to you, and those were the needs you were trying to take care of.'

It can also help to think of regret as being a coin with two sides, both of which need attention. On one side are my needs that weren't met by how I behaved, such as my longing to celebrate and support my colleague. These are the unmet needs that quickly gave rise to my judgemental thoughts about my selfishness. On the other side are my needs I was trying to meet in how I behaved, like wanting partnership on a meaningful project. Making sure I had connected empathically with all the needs on both sides of the coin helped me to see the situation in a clearer and more balanced way, and to find a way forward.

I then sent an email asking for another chance to discuss the plan, explaining that I hadn't been as whole-hearted in my celebration of the funding bid as I would have liked, and how delighted I was that my colleague had submitted it. I also said how excited I was about the project, and how important it was for me to progress it with them. In reply I received a warm email, and we had a much more productive conversation the second time around.

How might things have gone if I *hadn't* given myself some empathy and addressed my needs? I may have fired off a tetchy email and then felt bad about it. I might have sent a grovelling message, apologising excessively for my behaviour (thereby drawing my attention away from my client's feelings and towards my own). Or I might have avoided emailing at all, worrying that they would think I was selfish and rude, and so have stalled progress on the project.

PAUSE BOX

Explore the two sides of regret

Have to hand: the list of needs, and a pen and paper.

Jot down three headings on your paper: Judgemental Thoughts, Feelings, Needs.

1. Recall a moment when you acted in a way that you later regretted. What was it that you did or said?

2. Put on your needs glasses and, if you find it helpful, call your imaginary friend to remind you that everything you did, whether it seems that way or not, was an attempt to meet needs.

3. Connect with the feelings and judgemental thoughts you had, and note them down.

4. Coin 'heads': ask yourself which of your needs you didn't meet with your regretted behaviour. Make sure that you're looking at your own needs, not the needs of anybody who's been affected by your actions. In my situation it was 'celebration' (of my colleague), and 'collaboration' (shared working).

5. Coin 'tails': ask yourself what needs you were attempting to meet with your regretted behaviour. In my situation it was something like 'partnership' (working with others matters a lot to me), 'stimulation' (the project was exciting), and 'contribution' (to something I believed in).

6. Notice your feelings – is there any shift in how you feel when you connect with the needs you were trying to meet?

7. Having connected with your needs, ask yourself whether there's any action you want to take.

Guilt and shame can crush us. They take up space in our heads and hearts, so there's no room for healthy regret and an honest desire to change the way we behave. Needs Understanding offers us a way to move beyond guilt and find a way forwards, compassionately remembering that everything we do is an attempt to meet our needs.

If you only take one thing from this chapter...

- If you can apply self-compassion and identify your underlying needs in difficult situations, you can transform your life.

And if you take a few more...

- When you proactively fill your resource tank, you can be more available to both yourself and others.

- When you're triggered by someone or something, you're likely to be reacting to unmet fingerprint needs. If you give yourself time to rebalance, you'll be able to see and accept the needs that led to your strong feelings, allowing you to deal with the situation in a constructive way.

- When you do something that you later regret, it's because you were trying to meet your needs. Seeing your actions in this light allows you to have compassion for yourself, so you're better able to put things right.

Speak to BE HEARD

Part Three

Now we move on to how you can communicate in ways that hold everyone's needs with care. Key to this is building and maintaining a sense of connection with other people, so that whatever the outcome, your relationship is protected or even strengthened.

Chapter 6

Connect through speaking: creating conversations without barriers

- Creating conversations that connect you with others
- Talking about your needs in ways that get your message across
- Expressing your feelings so that you can build understanding
- Shifting from blame to freedom by changing your 'because'

Chapter 7

Four powerful tools for speaking: getting your point across

- Tool 1: observations not evaluations
- Tool 2: requests not demands
- Tool 3: appreciation and celebration, not praise and reward
- Tool 4: regret and sorrow, not guilt and denial

Chapter 6

Connect through speaking

Creating conversations without barriers

So far, we've explored how to empathise with both ourselves and others so that we can understand all the needs alive in a situation. Now we're looking at how we can speak in ways that take everyone's needs into consideration.

Whenever we speak, we give a voice to our underlying needs, and how we choose to do it makes it more or less likely that we'll communicate those needs. In other words, that we'll be fully heard. If we talk in a way that creates a barrier between us and the other person, it's as if we've built a wall. But if we speak in ways that build connection, we can lower the wall, leaving space for a free flow of understanding.

When I visit a formal organisation for work I'll wear a suit, not because I feel the need to blend in or because I particularly like wearing one, but because it's what I imagine will make it easiest for the people there to hear my message. I'm not inadvertently building a wall between me and them through what I wear. When I speak with someone it's the same thing. I want to decrease the likelihood of raising a wall of defensiveness or anger through what I say, even if our views don't coincide. That isn't the same as burying my ideas and opinions or keeping quiet – I certainly want to be heard. I can still be angry or forceful when I choose to be, but I try to talk in a way that makes it easier for people to hear and understand what's important to me.

In this chapter we'll look at ways of speaking that can help to lower the wall:

- creating conversations that connect you with others;

- talking about your needs in ways that get your message across;

- expressing your feelings so that you can build understanding; and

- shifting from blame to freedom by changing your 'because'.

These tools are designed to help create fruitful and collaborative conversations that are not only a lot more enjoyable than you may have had before, but that also have the potential to solve problems that have been troubling you for years. A subtle change in the way we speak can have a profound effect.

Creating conversations that connect you with others

Connection with people often comes automatically when you laugh together, joke, cry, share common interests or talk about your day. But what happens when you sense that you're grating on someone's nerves, or suspect you're not being understood? When connection doesn't come easily it can be helpful to have ways of making the dialogue work for both parties. Here are some pointers for generating connecting conversations.

Check you're resourced enough to be talking

Often, we launch into tricky conversations without taking a moment to ask ourselves if we're in the right frame of mind to talk. If you find this happens with you, you may want to check in with yourself first – it may mean the difference between having a conversation that works, and one that makes everyone feel unhappy. Here are some questions you can ask yourself before you speak, to see how resourced you are:

- Am I insistent on getting my own way?

- Are my emotions in control of me?

- Am I having judgemental thoughts?

- Do I want to make the other person suffer?

- Am I looking for them to fix my problems?

- Am I short of time or energy?

The more 'yes' answers you give, the less likely the other person is to hear you; they may become defensive and be more interested in protecting their own position than in understanding yours. The solution? 'Yeses' are a sign that you have unmet needs, so think about connecting with your needs and taking care of them before speaking with others. Once you've empathised with yourself, you'll be more likely to put yourself across clearly and compassionately.

Listen first to the other person's experience before speaking about your own

When you come to a difficult conversation, empathising with the other person first is usually likely to lower the wall of disconnection. Once they feel heard, they're better set up to listen to your message.

Make the conversation a dance

A connected conversation is like a dance – each person plays a role in creating the flow of movement. If you tend to talk a lot, notice the conversational space you're taking up – could you be monopolising the floor? If you're quiet for much of the time, are you still engaged in the conversation or have you withdrawn your attention, making the dance a little one-sided? A rewarding dance doesn't mean that each person needs to speak for an equal number of minutes. Some of us are naturally less talkative than others, and some conversations work well when one person speaks a lot and the other listens. It's more to do with having an awareness of the quality of your talking or listening, and aiming for both people's needs to be met in the conversation.

Use authentic language

In a moment you'll see some suggested types of words and phrases that you can use to connect through speaking. However, it's key that you use language that feels authentic to you. The most important element of all this is your intention. When your intention is to connect with others with care for both yourself and them, it doesn't really matter which words you use. Also, it's easy to become stuck in your head rather than your heart, and this is unlikely to lead to a productive conversation. So please take my suggestions only as a guide, and where they don't fit, use them to explore what language works better for you.

Talking about your needs in ways that get your message across

Because all human beings have both needs and feelings, they're two universal connectors between us. And because Needs Understanding is all about building connection, bringing needs and feelings into your conversations can be incredibly effective in removing barriers. This makes it less likely that you'll be misunderstood, and more likely that what's important to you will be heard. We'll explore how to talk about your needs here, and in a moment we'll move on to talking about your feelings.

When you're in a discussion with someone, talking about your needs can be powerful. It can sometimes be as straightforward as saying, 'I need stability' or 'I need purpose'. At other times though, you might want to use the following ideas to help you talk about your needs.

Express your needs in a way that's authentic for you

Many of us aren't used to communicating our needs in an overt way, so to pick a need from the list of needs and say 'I need truth' or 'I need understanding' can feel a bit forced or odd. There are a couple of approaches that can help with this.

The first is to use alternatives to 'I need', such as:

- I love [need]
- I value [need]

- I enjoy [need]
- I'd like [need]
- I could do with some [need]
- I'm hoping for [need]
- I care about [need]
- I thrive on [need]

Then you can add your need; for instance, 'I'd love to feel secure.' Alternatively, you can put the need first and then add words, such as:

- [need] is important to me
- [need] is fun for me
- [need] helps me feel happy
- [need] helps me feel well
- [need] matters to me

For instance, 'Harmony matters to me.'

The second approach is to ground your need in the context of what's going on at the time. This adds meaning and flexibility to what you say, depending on how you express it.

'Fun matters to me,' becomes

'It matters to me that we can joke around and have fun with each other.'

'I'd love to have a sense of support,' becomes

'I'd love each of us in our team to feel able to speak up when we're struggling, and to know that we'll support one another.'

Talk about your needs, not your judgemental thoughts

When someone has done something that we don't like, we might want to let them know the impact it's had on us. But how can we do that in a way that makes it most likely that we'll be heard? Without Needs Understanding, we might be tempted to make accusations.

'You never organise anything on time!'

'You can't be trusted to do what you say!'

'You're always shutting down my ideas!'

But from a Needs Understanding perspective, the other person hasn't done anything 'wrong'. What they've done is try to meet their needs – the problem being that they've done it in a way that doesn't take care of ours at the same time.

In Part Two (Understand yourself with compassion), we saw how judgemental thoughts like those above can be valuable signposts to our underlying needs. While we can warmly welcome judgemental thoughts to help us discover our needs, it's rarely helpful if they turn into spoken words. The other person, hearing the blame in our voices, will likely become defensive, and a wall will spring up between us. Our connection will be blocked, and they'll be less likely to hear what we want to say.

So how can we express ourselves without watering down our feelings, and at the same time make it more likely that our listener will hear how we've been affected? The key is to use the universal nature of human needs. If we name the needs that were affected by the other person's actions, our message can find a way through more easily.

'*You never organise anything on time,*' becomes

'*I need to be clear about our arrangements so I can plan my day.*' (expressing a need for clarity)

'*You can't be trusted to do what you say!*' becomes

'*Having trust in our relationship is really important to me.*' (expressing a need for trust)

'*You're always shutting down my ideas!*' becomes

'*It matters to me that I can be creative in our meetings.*' (expressing a need for creativity)

You can still feel angry or frustrated, but instead of talking about your judgements you're talking about your needs. When I went swimming with my teenage daughter recently, we were in the changing rooms and were about to get undressed, when she rounded on me out of the blue. 'Mum, can you get your bag off my peg? You're really annoying me – get out of my way!' Astonished, I turned to look at her. Where had that come from? Then a half smile crept up the side of her face. 'Mum, I may not have eaten that snack you left out for me this morning. I'm really hungry. Sorry.' After her initial outburst, she had managed to catch herself expressing blaming thoughts towards me. She could then look at what was going on for her underneath and connect her anger to her unmet need for food.

Talk about your needs, not your preferred strategy for meeting them

Suppose your son wants to play with you, which you'd love to do, but first you need to refill your internal resource tank after a stressful day. Your strategy is to take a bath. Without Needs Understanding you might say, 'I'm just going to take a bath and then I'll play with you.' If you're lucky your son might accept your suggestion, but it's just as likely that he'll get frustrated and you'll miss the chance of having fun with him.

Given that a listener is more likely to hear you when you talk about your needs rather than your preferred strategy for meeting them, you can choose to highlight your needs instead. 'I'd love to play with you, and I really need to look after myself after a long day so I get some energy back. I'll jump into the bath and be with you in 15 minutes. How's that for you?' You've described your underlying need for self-care, rather than only your strategy for meeting it. Of course, your son might still not accept this, but you have a better chance of being heard than if you'd only talked about your solution.

'*I can't join you for dinner tonight, as I have to finish this report first,*' becomes

'*I'd love to have dinner with you, but if I don't finish this report I'll be worrying about it all evening. Would it be okay if we met tomorrow night? Then we can really enjoy focusing on each other?*' (expressing a need for connection or intimacy)

'*I can't even think about booking a holiday until we've paid the bills,*' becomes

'*I'd love to have fun looking at holidays with you! I'm worried about how much we'll have to spend – could we sort out our bills first so that I can relax?*' (expressing a need for fun)

Talk about your needs, not your disguised demands

Keep an eye out for 'I need' followed by 'you' rather than a needs word, because that's usually the start of a demand. For instance, 'I need you to talk to him,' is a demand, whereas 'I need some peace of mind. Would you be prepared to speak to him?' is a direct expression of the need underlying your original words. It reveals your vulnerability, and is more likely to receive the answer 'yes' (or at least to open a conversation) than to raise a wall between you.

'To complete this project I'll need you to assign two more engineers,' becomes

'I want to get this project finished easily and with everyone on board. How about we bring on two more engineers?' (expressing a need for ease or cooperation)

'I'll need you to help out more around the house if we're to have another baby,' becomes

'I'd love to have another baby too, and I'm worried it will be more than I can manage. I want to do a good job of looking after our family. Can we talk about how to manage the workload around the house?' (expressing a need for support)

Sometimes you need to use more words when you express yourself in these ways, especially in situations when you don't have the luxury of the shorthand that comes with knowing someone well. However, in my experience it helps enormously with the connection you can build, and how much time you save further down the line.

PAUSE BOX

Unearth the needs behind your strategy

Have to hand: a pen and paper (if you want).

Suppose you want your son, daughter, partner, friend, or manager to do something. Think about what it could be.

What would it mean for you if they did what you wanted? What needs of yours would be met?

You may find that the situation is more about your own needs and less about what the other person should be doing.

Have a mini brainstorm about how to meet your needs. In the end, you might realise that you don't want the other person to do anything after all. Or you might now see how you can ask for what you need, but with a different energy – one that doesn't demand something from them, but instead helps them to see how they can help you if they'd like to.

Expressing your feelings so that you can build understanding

Feelings are a second universal connector because, like needs, we all have them. And although someone from one culture might think or speak about a feeling in a different way to another, the physical sensations that come along with them are universal. When another person says they're sad, joyful, or relieved, we can relate to what they mean and can empathise with them. It's a 'way in' to what we want to say, and helps us to move back and forth between their island and ours in a respectful and productive conversation.

You might sometimes find it difficult to talk about your feelings because you're worried they'll run away with you, or stop you being calm and logical. You might want to hide them, in the hope that your listener won't know that they're there. Or you might feel that you can't express them safely in a particular context like at work, or in a certain relationship.

But because feelings are such a strong connection point with others, it follows that people will pay your feelings as much (or maybe more) attention than if you were open about them. If you think about how you react when you sense that someone's angry or on edge, it's clear that you just know it, and the less it's acknowledged the more of your attention it risks attracting. In other words, if you don't talk about your feelings, it doesn't make them irrelevant to the situation; instead, they come out 'sideways'. What you can learn to do is to find ways of expressing them that fit for you in different areas of your life.

How to express your feelings

This can be as simple as saying, 'I feel tired' or 'I feel confused' (you can go to the list of feelings at the end of the book for inspiration).

Another option, if it feels more natural to you, is to say, 'I am' rather than 'I feel'.

'I am pleased.'

'I'm angry.'

'I was frightened.'

You can also use words for physical sensations, alone or in combination with feelings words.

'I feel numb.'

'I feel energised and excited.'

'I feel churned up with anger.'

Again, you can go to the end of the book to find the list of physical sensations to help.

False feelings

When you're talking about your feelings, it's important to keep an eye out for 'false feelings', or words that seem like feelings but aren't. These are subtle judgements of other people's behaviour. Our feelings are only to do with our inner experience, not our interpretation of what someone has done.

'*I feel sad*' is a direct description of how you feel – a reflection of what's happening inside you.

'*I feel rejected*' describes a feeling mixed up with a thought. It comes from a story you've created that runs like this: 'I have feelings of sadness because you ignored me.'

There are two issues to be aware of when you give voice to false feelings. The first is that they may show that you're stuck in a place of disempowerment or victimhood as a result of your thinking. Here your focus is on blaming someone else for your feelings, which means that you risk missing what you can do to change the situation yourself. That doesn't mean you have to ignore behaviour you don't like. What it does mean is that you can stop making your happiness dependent on the other person changing (which may or may not happen). Instead, you can connect with your needs, and harness your own power to make change.

The second issue with expressing false feelings is that the other person is less likely to listen to the message you want to put across, because they hear blame or judgement from you. To avoid this, consider replacing a false feeling word with a 'pure' feeling and an expression of your needs. In each of the following examples the second option is more likely to generate connection, whereas the first may raise a wall of defensiveness in your listener.

'*I feel let down by you,*' becomes

'*I feel sad! I really wanted to enjoy spending some time together.*' (expressing a feeling of sadness and a need for closeness)

'*I feel a bit overlooked,*' becomes

'*I feel disappointed because I put a lot of care into my proposal and would love some feedback. I'm wondering if you've had a chance to read it?*' (expressing a feeling of disappointment and a need for support or respect)

Here are some examples of false feelings (the list is also at the end of the book).

LIST OF FALSE FEELINGS

Abandoned	Insulted	Ripped off
Abused	Intimidated	Rushed
Attacked	Invalidated	Shunned
Belittled	Judged	Smothered
Betrayed	Left out	Suffocated
Blamed	Let down	Taken for granted
Boxed in	Manipulated	Trampled
Bullied	Misunderstood	Unappreciated
Cheated	Neglected	Unheard
Coerced	Overlooked	Unloved
Criticised	Overpowered	Unsupported
Diminished	Patronised	Used
Discounted	Pressured	Victimised
Hassled	Put down	Wronged
Ignored	Rejected	

Making the distinction between feelings and false feelings can take a bit of practice, but it can also be liberating. You're not trapped anymore by the belief that someone else is responsible for how you feel, which means that you can own your feelings instead. Also, by making that shift you remove the pressure from the other person, so they're less likely to feel defensive and more likely to understand what's going on for you.

PAUSE BOX

Find ways to move beyond false feelings

Have to hand: a pen and paper.

Notice how you and the people around you express their feelings, and jot them down. Which are 'pure' feelings and which are false ones? Notice when the expression combines implied feelings with some kind of judgement.

Being compassionately self-aware, consider the possibility of something else. Try out some different ways of expressing the feelings. Do they make you feel more or less connected with other people, and more or less empowered?

Shifting from blame to freedom by changing your 'because'

As we've seen in our exploration of false feelings, when someone does something we don't like, we may be inclined to make them responsible for how we feel. Another way of looking at this is to see that our feelings are never caused only by things or people outside of us.

Let's say that my father changes his plans at the last minute, which messes up my day. I find myself thinking, 'You're always doing this! It makes me really cross!' My focus is on the link between his actions and how I feel as a result. Or maybe I discover that my friend has been hiding something from me. Now my thoughts run along the lines of, 'Her not talking to me makes me sad. She doesn't think I'm a close enough friend.' Again, I'm seeing her actions as being the direct cause of my sadness.

This way of thinking and speaking can limit us. When we attribute our feelings directly to someone's actions, we become reliant on them changing their behaviour so that we can feel differently. And although we can ask them to change, we aren't in control of whether they do or not, so we limit our power to improve the situation.

There's a different way of thinking about this, which is that other people's behaviour is a *stimulus* for our feelings, rather than a direct cause. One way to understand this is to consider how your feelings about the same stimulus vary from day to day. On Monday morning your colleague not saying hello may irritate you, and on the next morning you feel relieved to have some peace and quiet. One day you're worrying about your child's progress at school, and on another it doesn't even enter your head. If it were the stimulus that was the direct cause of your feelings, you'd always feel the same about it. But you don't.

The missing piece in the picture is needs. Instead of focusing on the other person's actions, I can switch to how my needs give rise to my feelings. With my father changing plans, it might be that my need for consideration isn't met. And it may be my needs for connection and trust that aren't met when my friend hides something from me.

This helps me to change the situation in a constructive way. Instead of blaming my father for altering his plans and ending up in an argument, I'm free to look after my own needs in whatever way seems best. That might involve speaking to him in a manner that makes it likely he'll hear me, such as by talking about my feelings or needs, or it might end up with me meeting my need in some other way. With my friend who hid something from me, instead of blaming her for my hurt, I could talk to her in a non-judgemental way. Or I could realise that the situation has triggered a fingerprint need, which I can take care of myself.

PAUSE BOX

Explore the relationship between your feelings and people's actions

Have to hand: a pen and paper.

Think of a recent situation in which you felt angry with someone. Maybe your colleague didn't do his work, your partner was late again, or your mother gave you unasked-for advice.

Write a sentence that makes someone else responsible for your anger: 'I felt angry because [of what the person did].' For instance, 'I felt angry because he didn't contact me for three days!'

Read your sentence to yourself. See if you can gain a felt sense of the emotion you've described.

Now flip your sentence around to make your needs responsible for your anger: 'When [the person did that thing], I felt angry because I want/need/love (choose from the list of needs).' For instance, 'When he didn't contact me for three days, I felt angry because I long to be heard and to feel more connection with him.'

Notice any shift in your feelings as you do this. Does anything change when you see them as linked to your needs, rather than only to the other person's actions?

You could have a couple of goes with different scenarios, using different feelings.

Changing your 'because'

Separating someone's actions from your feelings also gives both you and them the freedom to act in each other's best interests. Taking the example of my father changing his plans, if I were to tell him, 'I feel frustrated because you changed your plans yet again,' I load him with the responsibility for how I feel. Instead of hearing helpful feedback about his behaviour, he's likely to feel guilt or resentment. What I want instead is for us to look together at how the situation isn't working for either of us, without blame attached.

A useful first step towards this is to change what you say, so that you link your feeling to your underlying need.

'I feel upset because you changed your plans,' becomes

'I feel upset because I want some consideration for the impact on me.' (expressing a need for consideration)

'I feel sad because you hid something important from me,' becomes

'I feel sad because it matters to me that we share things with each other.' (expressing a need for trust)

'I felt embarrassed when you read out my mistakes in the meeting,' becomes

'When you read out my mistakes in the meeting, I felt embarrassed because my relationship with the new partners is important to me.' (expressing a need for belonging or mutuality)

There's even a bit of a formula to this, in which

'I feel [feeling] because you [their action]' becomes

'I feel [feeling] because I need [your need].'

In the next chapter we'll look at four more language tools that will help you to speak in ways that build connection.

If you only take one thing from this chapter…

- When speaking with people, your main aim is to avoid building a wall that creates disconnection and separation, and instead to clear a space for connection and productive communication.

And if you take a few more...

- Talking about your needs and feelings can be an instant way to generate understanding because they're two universal connectors.

- False feelings are feelings that are mixed up with judgemental thoughts, and they can make it hard for other people to hear you.

- Approaching a situation with a focus on your underlying needs, rather than the desire for someone else's behaviour to change, can help you shift from feeling stuck to taking empowered action.

Chapter 7

Four powerful tools for speaking

Getting your point across

In the previous chapter, we explored what it means to create quality connections with people through speaking, mainly by using the universal connectors that all humans share: needs and feelings. Here, we'll build on that when we discover four further language tools that can help you to communicate in potentially difficult situations.

These tools are useful not only as practical possibilities for expressing yourself, but also as ways of helping you to become more aware of your thinking. When you see your thoughts in new ways, you're more able to change them if they're not working for you. Both uses of the tools can empower you to spend less time judging yourself and others, and more time achieving what you want in life.

Over the years, we develop habitual ways of thinking and speaking. When we look at each tool, we'll explore why these may be unhelpful, and how the Needs Understanding way can help with building trust and generating powerful solutions to intractable problems.

The tools are:

- making observations not evaluations;
- making requests not demands;
- offering appreciation and celebration, not praise and reward; and
- expressing regret and sorrow, not guilt and denial.

Tool 1: observations not evaluations

Observations are neutral statements of facts that everyone can agree on, whereas evaluations are your personal interpretations of those facts.

'You've been putting pressure on me!' is an evaluation.

'I've received three emails from you since yesterday,' is an observation.

'My partner isn't very affectionate,' is an evaluation.

'I notice my partner seems uncomfortable if I hold her hand or try to kiss her in public,' is an observation.

The way this tends to play out in life is that when someone does something that we don't like, our habitual response may be to feel upset and blame it on them. However, if our aim is for something to change, we need to be *heard* by the other person, and we're generally much better at responding positively when we hear observations rather than evaluations. Evaluations can throw up walls between people because the listener feels blamed. Observations involve no fault-finding, and make it easier for the listener to think about how the problem can be solved.

'You've left the living room in a mess!' is an evaluation. When someone hears that, they're likely to focus on justifying their behaviour, with the result that they don't hear what matters to us.

'I noticed there were books and papers on the living room floor,' is an observation. The person responsible is less likely to be caught up in defending themselves and more inclined to consider our experience of the situation.

'You don't trust me!' is an evaluation, and may provoke a defensive reply.

'When you ask me to show you my emails before I send them to the board, I find myself doubting whether you trust me,' is an observation. In this we're describing the action and owning our perspective on it, giving the other person something to work constructively with in response.

'You're late,' is an evaluation.

'You said you'd be back by 6:00pm,' is an observation. This is better because it's more factual, but there are two potential problems with it. The first is that if the other person doesn't think that they said they'd return by 6:00pm, it will open up a disagreement about who said what. The second is that the phrase 'you said' can be heard as an accusation, which may throw up a wall in its own right.

'I understood that you'd be back by 6:00pm,' or *'I heard you say that you'd be back by 6:00pm,'* are observations that are better still for keeping connection with the other person, because there can be no argument about our own perception of the situation. We're stating what we believe to be true.

Like other tools in this chapter and the last, you can use observations in writing as well as in speech. An email saying, *'I understood you'd reply by tomorrow,'* works better than one saying, 'You said you'd reply by tomorrow,' because it gives the opportunity for the recipient to respond with, 'Oh, that's not what I meant,' or 'Yes, I can see why you thought that.' Even if what you say doesn't reflect their memory of what was agreed, they can still see your point of view, and there's plenty of room for an amicable discussion about the way forward.

A friend of mine explored the use of observations when she was helping her parents to clear out their house. She took a collection of items to the recycling centre, and when she returned her mum asked, 'Where are the puddings? I told you they were in the box with the newspapers!' My friend felt a stab of annoyance. However, instead of replying, 'You didn't tell me there were puddings in the box!' as she usually would, she said, 'I have no memory of talking about puddings, but tell me about them and how I can help.' She wasn't accepting blame, but she wasn't blaming her mum either. A conversation about a shopping trip to replace the puddings then followed, which allowed them to sort the problem out.

What about 'positive' evaluations – aren't they okay?

It might seem counter-intuitive, but it's not only 'negative' evaluations that can lead to disconnection, but positive ones as well. That's because your positive observations will often be heard as supportive and helpful only if they agree with how the other person sees things.

For instance, a birth professional supported a woman during a difficult birth. She thought the mother had been incredible, and when she went back to visit her and the new baby, she said, 'You were amazing throughout the birth – so strong and calm. You're a natural at this.' Unexpectedly for the midwife, the mother became angry, telling her that she'd been terrified and had felt unable to move or speak for fear of falling to pieces.

Complimenting or appreciating someone can be a lovely way of connecting with them, but how you do it matters. Here, the birth professional saying something like, 'I thought you were so strong and calm through the birth – how did you feel?' might have given more room for them both to share their points of view.

Telling your friend, 'You're such a wonderful daughter,' builds connection if she's happy with how she's supporting her mum. On the other hand, if your friend thinks that she could be kinder to her, your comment may leave her feeling alone and unseen. Instead, you could try something like, 'I'm guessing your mum is loving all your extra visits at the moment.'

In each of these examples, the suggested alternatives for what to say involve being clear that it's a personal point of view, rather than it being the objective truth. This leaves space for the other person to talk about their own version of reality. We'll look more fully at what you can say instead of positive evaluations when we move on to appreciation and celebration later on in this chapter.

PAUSE BOX

Recognise your own evaluations

Have to hand: a pen and paper.

Think of something that happened to you recently and that stimulated a reaction in you – perhaps you felt embarrassed, angry, anxious, or delighted.

Take a moment to write freely about what happened without censoring yourself in any way.

When you've finished, go back and see if you have any evaluations – positive or negative – in what you've written. If so, try replacing a word or phrase with an observation.

Do you notice any shift in how you're now seeing the situation?

Tool 2: requests not demands

Being on the receiving end of a demand generally doesn't feel good. We tend either to comply with it grudgingly or to rebel against it, and a wall is created between us and the other person. It follows that when you're the one who wants someone else to do something, they're more likely to hear and help you if you make a request rather than a demand.

The difference between requests and demands isn't only about what words you use. It also involves recognising that your objective isn't to get your own way or to make the other person change, because you can't. What you can do, though, is to ask for what you want in a way that makes it most likely that they'll consider your request, recognising that whether or not they decide to meet it is entirely down to them.

Marshall Rosenberg put it like this when he talked about the folly of thinking that you can control your child's behaviour. 'You can't make your kids do anything. All you can do is make them wish they had. And then they will make you wish you hadn't made them wish they had.'[3] For 'kids', you could

---

[3] Marshall Rosenberg said this orally when he gave trainings. There's a longer version of it in his booklet *Raising Children Compassionately*, published by PuddleDancer Press.

substitute 'partner', 'employee', 'friend', or anyone else you want something from.

A request is a tool for letting someone know what you would like them to do to meet your needs, but only if it also meets theirs in the process. Your aim is to create the sort of connection with someone that leads them to want to attend to your needs as well as their own, and vice versa. In other words, requesting is one way of looking after the relationship at the same time as achieving what you want.

So what's the best way to make a request? Requests are usually more likely to maintain connection when they have these four main features. They're:

- specific;
- positive;
- honest and direct; and
- open to the possibility of a 'no'.

Let's look at each in turn.

Specific requests

Make your request as specific as possible so that each of you is clear about what you want.

'Will you come and see me more often?' becomes

'Would you be able to come and see me each month?'

'Could you make progress with the staff appraisals this week?' becomes

'Can you do two appraisals by Friday?'

Positive requests

Ask for what you do want, not for what you don't; this avoids any implication of blame.

'*Would you spend less time playing video games this evening?*' becomes

'*Would you be up for playing that new board game later tonight?*'

'*Please don't leave food in the staff fridge over the weekend,*' becomes

'*Please remember to take food out of the fridge on Friday.*'

Honest and direct requests

Ask for what you want openly, to avoid resentment building between you and the other person.

Whenever David's husband, Peter, wants David's help with his computer, he doesn't ask him directly but keeps telling him about what isn't working until David sorts it out. Peter feels guilty about taking up David's time, and fears that one day he'll refuse to help, so rather than asking him honestly he uses hints. In turn, David feels resentful because he doesn't sense any appreciation for his support. Instead, Peter could say, 'David, I need help with my computer again. Are you okay to spend a couple of hours on it on Saturday?'

Sarah's elderly mum does something similar: 'Be a dear and help me out around the house this afternoon, will you?' she says. Sarah feels irritation at this. 'Am I only a dear if I do what she asks? Am I even free to say no?' Sarah misses the connectedness and joy of being able to say 'yes' freely and without a sense that it's expected of her. She'd probably be more responsive to this request: 'Sarah, would you be able to help me change the sheets this afternoon? I'm starting to find them difficult to manage on my own.'

Requests that are open to the answer 'no'

The most important aspect of making a request, and often the hardest to accept, is being genuinely willing to hear a 'no'. Our habitual response when someone says 'no' to us can be to blame the other person, make them feel guilty, or punish them in some way. But when we do that, we put a strain on our relationship, building a wall of disconnection and reducing the other person's willingness to help us out. The best we can expect is that they'll do what we ask but only to avoid an argument, or that they'll say 'yes' and then not follow it through.

The key question to ask yourself before you make a request is, 'Am I open to hearing a no?' If you're not, then however specific, positive, and direct you're being, you're actually making a demand, and may find the other person reacting defensively. This can come across as much through your tone of voice as through the words you use; it's the intention and energy that makes the difference.

'We'll meet again to discuss this next week,' becomes

'I'd like to meet again next week to discuss this. Does that work for everyone?'

'Make sure you take the rubbish out,' becomes

'Are you okay to take the rubbish out?'

'Let's take a vote now,' becomes

'Does anyone have a concern about taking a vote now?'

Hearing 'no' to a request can be hard. When this happens you may want to take a moment to connect with your needs so that you don't react in habitual ways. Which of your needs aren't being met when you hear the 'no'? You can also move on to ask yourself about the other person's needs. What needs are they trying to meet when they say 'no'? Finally, it can help to see the word 'no' as the start of a conversation, not the end. If you move to a connecting conversation like the ones we explored in the last chapter, you can share your needs and look for solutions that work for everyone.

Recently, my friend Paul asked his sister Ella if she would help him out one Sunday with some maintenance at their elderly parents' house. There were some jobs that would need two people, and he'd previously told her how difficult they'd be without her support. Her response was 'no'. He was annoyed, but he went through the process in the paragraph above and started to see what was behind his knee-jerk response.

First, he empathised with himself. 'You know what?' he said to himself. 'I take on all of the care for our parents' house and garden, and I've done it with a bad back recently. I'd love some help and recognition for how much I do.' When he'd done that, he realised that he had a strong need for competence, which meant he hadn't opened up to his sister about his back pain. This acceptance of his own needs smoothed the way for him to think about what was going on for her. He remembered that she often worked six days a week, leaving Sunday as the only day to spend with her two young children. He guessed that her need was to spend quality time connecting with them, and that she was longing for him to see the goodwill behind her refusal.

At this point, Ella's 'no' became the start of a further conversation. Paul asked her if she'd be open to hearing about where he was coming from, and non-judgementally described his needs and the effect the situation was having on him. This encouraged her to share her side, which turned out to be that she was feeling stressed and had also promised her sons she would spend Sundays playing with them. She was intent on keeping this promise, but having connected with her brother and heard what was bothering him, decided to ask her boys if they would like a day out at their grandparents' house. They said they would. Paul booked a meal at a local pub, so they had time to work hard on the jobs and also share a happy hour out together in a way they hadn't for months. During the day they talked about how they could work together to support their parents in the future.

PAUSE BOX

Explore hearing a 'no'

Think of a time when someone said 'no' to you. Notice what you wanted the other person to do, and how this would have met your needs.

Then ask yourself, 'Was I ever okay to hear a 'no' from this person?'

Next, think about what, if anything, got in the way of you being okay with a 'no'. This may reveal other needs that were alive for you at the time, or some kind of belief about what you thought should be true.

How else could you have met your needs?

You may be wondering what to do if you've tried these approaches and the person you're asking still says 'no'. In that case you have a number of options. You can keep communicating with them about the impact it has on you. You can look for other ways to meet your needs. Or you can choose to make a demand. This may be your best option when it's essential to prioritise your own needs and you can't see any other way of meeting them. A demand can build a high wall between you and the other person, so you may want to pay particular attention to reconnecting with them once the situation has passed.

You may have relationships in which some of your needs are consistently unmet despite everything you've tried. When that's the case, you may choose to stay in the relationship because enough other needs are met, or – ultimately – you may want to re-evaluate whether you keep trying to build a connection with this person.

Tool 3: appreciation and celebration, not praise and reward

It was a sunny Tuesday afternoon, and I was waiting at the school gates for my daughter, then aged five, to arrive. Before long, she rushed out with her new friend Jayde. 'Look what Jayde's got, Mum! A sticker for being the best behaved in the whole class!' To provide evidence, Jayde proudly pointed to a smiley face stuck on her jumper. It was the first of many, many times over the years that my daughter has come home with evidence of the praise and reward culture that flourishes in our education system. I find it just as concerning now as I did when she was young.

What's my worry? It's that by rewarding children for things, we teach them to gear their behaviour to gain outside approval, rather than to satisfy their own inner values. That isn't to imply any criticism of teachers, whom I see doing a remarkable job with minimal resources. For me, it's a systemic issue that exists in our culture. At work, you've probably experienced bonus schemes, 'employee of the month' type programmes, or feedback in the form of verbal praise. At school it was stickers, house points, and prizes for winning at sports. And at home, you might have been promised treats or received a gift if you did what was expected of you.

Whether praise and rewards are bestowed by parents, managers, or others in positions of authority, they don't tend to lead to relationships built on trust, or foster closer connections. More often than not, they're well-meaning attempts to manipulate our behaviour so that it conforms to what other people want. Even more harmfully, they can encourage us to change what we do so that we'll win a reward for it, rather than giving us the freedom to act from a genuine desire to do what meets our needs and those of the people around us. In Jayde's case, her sticker was unlikely to have helped her to think about why it would be useful to behave with consideration for others, or to reflect on whether or not her behaviour met her needs. I wanted her to be asking herself, 'What kind of person do I want to be?' rather than, 'How do I get more stickers?'

And yet surely it's a good thing to help people feel positive about themselves when they've achieved something worthwhile? Aren't rewards a helpful way to socialise children into the behaviour we want to see? Of course, I want people to like who they are, and I definitely want children to develop caring and thoughtful behaviour, but not at the expense of harmful consequences. As we continue to receive reward and praise throughout our lives, we can become competitors with our colleagues, siblings, and classmates, rather than holding everyone's needs with care. We build walls rather than taking them down. And because of the dependence we've been taught to have on external validation for our sense of self-worth, we crave the approval of others rather than knowing how to value ourselves. We may hold back from trying new things or experimenting creatively because it doesn't feel safe. What if we fail? How will we feel good about ourselves then?

This manipulative aspect of praise and reward becomes clear when you consider that it's not something you would give to a friend, or a person whom you're not in a position of authority over. If your best friend gained a promotion or got engaged, for instance, you'd celebrate with them rather than rewarding them: 'Let's go for a drink and toast your good news!' Here it's not about a sticker or a badge, but about leaping into your friend's joy at their own success.

So what are the possible alternatives to praise and reward? Naturally, whether you're managing a team that's achieved extraordinary results, or parenting a child who's learned something new, you want to show your delight and share in the pleasure of their accomplishments. The key is to examine your motives. If you're giving praise to your team at work to encourage them to repeat their success the following month, or to your child so they work equally hard at school tomorrow, you're in the realm of incentives and may want to consider keeping quiet. If, on the other hand, you want to delight in whatever's happened, you could choose one of the following options.

Three alternatives to praise

Celebration: stand (or jump!) alongside the person. Here, you're sharing in their feelings about their achievement, rather than imposing your own judgement of it. As ever, it's the intention you convey that's more important than the words you use; you can take your lead from the person you're celebrating with.

Parent: *'Well done for doing so well in your maths test. That deserves an ice cream!'* becomes

Parent: *'I'm so pleased!! Wow, are you excited? Tell me more!'*

Appreciation: say what the person did and which needs it met for you. Now you're owning the impact on you, rather than judging their behaviour according to an external standard.

'You've been so good and quiet all morning,' becomes

'I really appreciate you finding games to play on your own this morning – it's lovely to have my work done so I can enjoy the rest of the weekend.'

This way, the other person receives feedback about how their behaviour has helped you. If they repeat it, it's likely to be because they've enjoyed contributing to you, rather than for some external reward.

Say what you see: describe what you see in the other person and ask them what they notice. Doing this encourages them to form their own judgement of themselves or their work, rather than you offering your own up front.

'That was a great presentation you did to the CEO. I'll remember that when I do your appraisal next month,' becomes

'I noticed the CEO was nodding and writing lots of notes in your presentation. How do you feel it went?'

PAUSE BOX

Explore the link between appreciation and needs

Have to hand: the list of needs, and a pen and paper.

Think of something that a person did that you enjoyed. Perhaps an old friend phoned out of the blue, a colleague came to you for advice, or your teenager unexpectedly did the washing up without being asked.

Use your list of needs to see which needs were met for you.

Next, look back over this section and write down what you might say if you wanted to express your appreciation to them.

Tool 4: regret and sorrow, not guilt and denial

In Chapter 5 (How to unlock difficult situations), we looked at how, when we do something we later regret, we were only trying to meet our needs. We explored ways, after the event, of connecting with both the needs we failed to meet and the needs we were trying to meet. Here we'll take this one step further by exploring how we might express regret to someone who's been hurt through our behaviour. It's important to know how to do this, as unless we apologise in a way that takes care of everyone's needs (including our own), we can fall into one of two traps:

- we bury our guilt by becoming defensive, or denying that we need to apologise at all; or

- we feel overwhelmed by guilt, and grovel in an effort to make the other person forgive us so that we can feel good about ourselves again.

The 'sorry' we're talking about in Needs Understanding aims to make amends in a way that deals with the fall-out from the incident *and* puts in place what's needed to move forward. It's all about restoring the relationship.

How 'sorry' works in Needs Understanding

Here are some ways of saying sorry that are likely to lower the wall that's been raised. They're not in any particular order, so please feel free to pick and choose what fits for you.

Say sorry empathically. An apology that helps to build connection might include:

- being clear about what you're apologising for;

- having empathy for the other person's position; and

- saying what you'll do differently next time, or asking them what they'd like you to do differently.

'I'm really sorry I said that about you in the meeting. I can see how you might feel upset and angry. Would you like to say more about how it was for you? Or is there anything you'd like me to do now?'

How does this differ from conventional ways of apologising? It's because you're not doing it from a place of wrongness but from a place of sadness. With your needs glasses on you can see yourself with compassion and understanding, which helps you to take into account the impact you've had. All the time, you were only trying to meet your needs.

Allow the other person to express their feelings if they want to. Listen with empathy, and avoid interrupting, defending yourself, or arguing. If you notice yourself becoming reactive, take a moment to offer yourself some understanding and empathy before turning your focus back to the other person. At the same time, try not to allow yourself to be pitched back into a place of guilt from which you want them to rescue you. This is about them, not you.

Take ownership of your mistakes. This is not the same as blaming yourself. Blame not only has a harmful effect on you, but it also makes it difficult for you to empathise with how the other person has been affected.

It can help to remember that you and the other person each has a different focus. They want the impact of your actions on them to be heard, while you're likely to want to make your intentions clear – why you acted as you did. You can build your ability to make meaningful apologies by first turning to yourself, acknowledging the reasons for your actions, and making peace with yourself. The more you understand yourself, the less likely you are to try to get the other person to show understanding to you, and the more available you are to hear the effect of your actions on them.

'*I didn't mean to upset you when I sent that message!*' becomes

'*I'm hearing how much my message affected you, and I'm really sorry. In retrospect, I wish I hadn't sent it.*'

Don't say 'I'm sorry but…' If you add a 'but', you're defending yourself rather than apologising.

'*I'm sorry I was slow to respond, but I've just had so much on this week,*' becomes

'*I'm sorry I was slow to respond. I can see how that was a problem for you.*'

After you've apologised, and only if the other person wants to listen, you can tell them what was going on for you. When you do this, it's helpful to remember the tools for connected conversations that we explored in the last chapter, such as talking about the feelings and needs that motivated your behaviour.

The problem with guilt

It's easy to become mired in guilt when we've done something we regret. But by doing this we tend to focus unintentionally on ourselves, rather than on the other person. It's as if we have an agenda for them to forgive us so that we can feel better. One example is a friend of mine who, as part of his reconciliation with himself as a gay man, separated from his wife after 30 years of marriage. When he thought of the impact on her he was consumed by guilt. It was only when he was able to move past the guilt that he could be fully present to what was going on for his wife.

'I'm so sorry – I feel absolutely dreadful about what happened. I've behaved so terribly,' becomes

'I'm so very sorry. I imagine it must have been really hard for you. Tell me more about it?'

If you only take one thing from this chapter…

- Difficult conversations, such as saying what isn't working for us or asking someone to do something differently, don't have to end in disagreement; in fact, there are ways of handling them that can both build closer connections and produce creative solutions.

And if you take a few more…

- When we're not happy with someone, making an observation rather than an evaluation helps us to challenge their behaviour without harming the relationship.

- If we want something, we can't make someone give it to us; instead, we can make a thoughtful request.

- Praise and reward, while seeming helpful, can have unintended harmful effects; appreciation and celebration are more effective at building connections with others.

- When we want to make amends for something we've done, guilt and denial block us from focusing on the other person; instead, we can get in touch with our sadness and regret to help us repair the relationship.

Act with care for everyone's NEEDS

Part Four

In Part One we looked at connecting with other people's needs through empathy; in Part Two we explored connecting with our own needs; and in Part Three we focused on how we can talk about all the needs at play in a situation. The fourth skill area of Needs Understanding centres on what we can do with this knowledge.

Chapter 8

Your needs, my needs, and a new way forward: creating strategies that work for everyone

- The needs dip
- A practical framework for holding everyone's needs with care
- Examples of how the framework can work
- Isn't this another way of talking about compromise?
- Holding onto needs and letting go of strategies
- When hidden fingerprint needs hold the key to solutions
- Using the framework with internal dilemmas

Chapter 9

Beyond right and wrong: moving from opposition to collaboration

- The opposition paradigm
- The partnership paradigm
- Respectful boundaries – saying 'no' with care
- Connecting across divides

Chapter 8

Your needs, my needs, and a new way forward

Creating strategies that work for everyone

This is where everything we've looked at comes together. We've explored how to sense all the needs in a situation, and discovered ways of connecting with people by talking about those needs so that we can build closer and more productive relationships. But what happens next? How do you deal with it when you want one thing and someone else wants something different? How can you find a way to hold everyone's needs with care, but at the same time keep what's important to you?

This is where it can be helpful to have a simple framework that you can use in any situation for finding ways forward that are likely to work for everyone. We'll start off by looking at how the framework brings together everything that we've covered so far, and also helps with putting Principle 2 of Needs Understanding into practice: our world works best when our chosen strategies take care of everyone's needs. Then we'll explore how you can apply it in a practical way, using a range of scenarios that cover different aspects of holding everyone's needs with care. The outcomes from these include coming up with win-win solutions rather than lose-lose compromises, achieving what you want in difficult situations without causing problems in your relationships, and moving past personal blocks to find a more creative way forward.

The needs dip

You may remember that in Chapter 1 (The surprisingly simple secret) we looked at how we tend to leap straight from problem to strategy without considering the needs at play in a situation. That's fine if everyone is happy with the strategy that's decided upon. For instance, if a manager and his employee agree that they've both got into an unhealthy habit of working overly long hours (the problem) and jointly decide to encourage each other to leave the office by 5:30pm (the strategy), they've probably taken their needs into account without even realising it. The underlying needs might be different for each, but the solution is a mutually happy one and there's no need to think about it any further.

But what happens when life isn't so easy? What if the manager thinks that the solution is to work more efficiently, but the employee considers themselves already to be overburdened and wants a reduced workload? In that case, it's easy to see how leaping straight from problem to strategy could end in a disagreement. There might be a power struggle, with the manager asserting their authority by imposing their own solution, or an uneasy compromise that doesn't really work for either party.

A more productive way through this is to 'dip down' into the needs at play before deciding what to do about the problem.

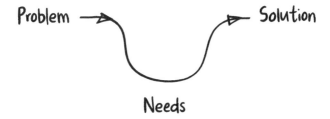

You may remember this diagram from the beginning of the book. The idea behind it is that people's strategies can conflict, but the needs underlying them are universal. This universality enables us to recognise where other people are coming from. When you're able to consider and connect with both their needs and your own, you can usually find solutions that work for everyone.

At the same time, you might recall the 'needs pot' that we also talked about in the first chapter. The process of dipping down into needs is a bit like putting everyone's needs into a cooking pot, giving them a stir, and seeing what comes out. This helps you to see each situation in a unique way, and to come up with fresh and creative strategies that last for the long term. It takes a bit more time than jumping to a solution, but it's so much more nourishing than a 'fast food' fix.

A practical framework for holding everyone's needs with care

So much for analogies. Given that we clearly don't have an actual pot that we can put the needs into, how can we best 'hold everyone's needs with care'? What does it mean in reality? When I share the framework in workshops, I usually start by introducing it as a physical process that involves stepping from one place to another. I'm going to present it like that here, but please feel free to do whatever helps you most to get familiar with it. Instead of walking it through, you may prefer to map it out on a piece of paper, or simply go through the steps in your head.

If you'd like to walk through an example now as you read, then have a pen and six sheets of paper to hand and label them as follows:

- Situation

- My Feelings

- My Judgemental Thoughts

- My Needs

- Other Person's Needs

- Strategy

Arrange them on the floor according to the diagram below, with you standing beside the Situation sheet. (I'll also refer to the list of needs, which you can find at the end of the book).

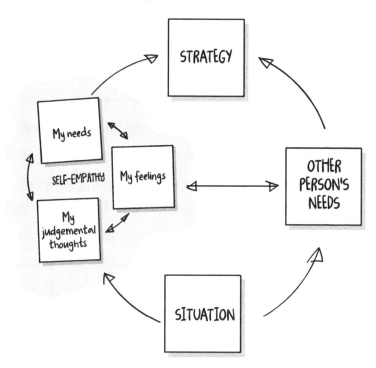

Next, describe to yourself a difficult situation that's troubling you. It might be a current problem, something that happened in the past, or a future scenario you're worried about. As ever, the first time you try this out it's best to pick something that's not too emotionally intense. As you recall the situation, you may find your thoughts coming out in a bit of a jumble, or you may find it easy to think with clarity – it doesn't matter. The main thing is to take a moment to connect with what's going on and how it's affecting you. If you notice feelings coming up for you, take the time you need to remind yourself that allowing your feelings is a natural and healthy part of the process.

I'm now going to invite you to shift to a different way of thinking about your problem. Try turning to your left and looking at the triangle of pieces of paper labelled My Feelings, My Judgemental Thoughts, and My Needs. Walk over to them and stand in front of them. Choose one of the three to step on and see what comes up for you; most people find it easiest to first choose either My Feelings or My Judgemental Thoughts because, as we know from Part Two (Understand yourself with compassion), these are two main signposts to your needs. Can you name any feelings you have right now? And what about your judgemental thoughts? We don't tend to acknowledge these to ourselves because we can feel ashamed of them, but the aim here is to welcome them with compassion and to try to connect with the needs that they're signalling.

As a way of helping with this, I suggest that you look at the list of needs. Why not take a moment to read it through and see if there are any that jump out at you? What needs are alive for you right now? It's at this moment that something transformational can happen: 'Of course! I'm upset because I'm exhausted and want someone to appreciate how hard I'm trying. I need recognition, rest, and understanding.' You might feel a physical sense of relief wash over you, as these needs become clear.

It's useful to bear in mind that sometimes it's easy to come up with needs that aren't really needs; for instance, 'I just need her to be on time instead of running late every day.' If your need isn't on the list, it might be that what you've identified is your *preference* for meeting your underlying needs, rather than a universal need that we all share. A preference is just your preferred strategy in the situation. To help you distinguish between a preference and a need, you can ask yourself what need would be met for you if you got what you wanted. Here your *preference* is for your colleague to be on time, whereas your *need* might be for respect or consideration. It's the process of connecting with your true needs, rather than preferences, that usually shifts situations most powerfully.

Now it's time to walk to the Other Person's Needs so that you can start to build a mental and emotional connection with them. Can you take a guess at what might be going on for them? What might their needs be? Of course, they're not there to ask or to listen to empathically right now, but the act of crossing over to their island and thinking about the problem from their perspective can take you several steps closer to understanding them with compassion. Try to describe what you think their needs could be.

It's at this stage that you can move towards a strategy. Many people find that this becomes easy and obvious once they've been through the process of identifying the needs at play, but if it isn't, don't worry. You might need more time for the solution to come to you, or it could be that your immediate strategy is to have an empathic conversation with the other person and come up with a solution together. Whatever the outcome, it's likely to be a more constructive one than anything you would have thought of without sensing the underlying needs first.

This process can be flexible. If you're simply feeling confused about why someone is behaving in a certain way, for instance, you might go straight to the Other Person's Needs and leave out your own. Their behaviour isn't a problem to you, it's just that you'd like to understand it. Also, you can go back and forth between the cards as often as you like; as we saw in Chapter 4 (What makes you tick?), the reason for Needs, Feelings, and Judgemental Thoughts being in a triangle is so that you can move between them in whatever direction works for you. I encourage you to keep stepping around – it's not a linear process. The only direction that matters is the one from Situation to Strategy *via* Needs and not directly.

In summary

This framework contains four basic steps (with steps two and three being interchangeable in order):

1. Describing the situation

2. Connecting with your needs by exploring your own island

3. Connecting with the other person's needs by visiting theirs

4. Coming to a strategy

It helps to practise this process when you're out of the moment so that you get used to it and find it easier to carry out when you're in it. You might want to revisit an argument with your partner, or be able to look forward to a difficult meeting at work which you're dreading. You can use it to understand more of what was (or is) going on for you and for others, and to find new strategies for making progress. Using this framework can help you to switch your focus from the stories you tell yourself that keep you stuck, and towards the needs that are alive in a situation. That's how you can transform problems into creative, workable solutions.

Examples of how the framework can work

Sometimes it's easiest to see how something works through examples, so here are a couple of stories that illustrate the method playing out in real life.

The first features my cousin Annabel, who's in her mid-twenties and has recently moved into a shared house. It was already occupied by four people who knew each other well, so Annabel was conscious of being the 'new girl' at first. She got on with them all, but there was a problem and she didn't know how to deal with it. It seemed that while they wanted to live without the heating on most of the time, she was freezing cold and longing to turn up the thermostat by several notches. It was about more than just being uncomfortable. Annabel had lived in a cold, damp house in the past and had become ill as a result; as a professional dancer, she had to look after her body if she was to work and pursue her passion. She became more and more worried and upset about the situation, but didn't want to force her housemates to turn on the heating and upset the friendships she was just starting to forge.

One of them, Ezra, was the most adamant about keeping the heating off. By chance, Annabel found herself alone with him in the kitchen one morning, and decided to talk to him about it. She knew that arguing her case by making him feel guilty about the heating would be unlikely to land them in a good place longer term, so she focused on voicing her feelings instead. 'I'm frightened,' she blurted out. 'I really am. I got ill when I lived in a cold house before, and as a dancer I can't afford that again. It's too important to me.'

Ezra was shocked – he hadn't realised that she felt scared (in fact, until that moment nor had Annabel), and was touched by the vulnerability he saw. This opened up a space for him to talk about his fears as well. 'I'm worried about money,' he said. 'My work is so up and down, I never know if I'll have enough to pay the bills from one month to the next. I guess I see the heating costs as something I can control.'

Because of their willingness to let their guards down and open up about their feelings, both Annabel and Ezra saw that they wanted to help one another. Annabel had a need for health, Ezra for security, and both had a need for connection with each other. This allowed them to shift their positions, with Ezra's anxiety about meeting his need for security lessening as he identified more with Annabel's need for health. 'Of course I want you to stay well so you can do your dancing,' he said. 'I'm sure we can find a way of managing the heating that we're both happy with.' In turn, Annabel took Ezra's money concerns seriously and promised to see if they could find a way of not running up huge bills. In the end, they decided to have the heating on full time for a month and to analyse the bill at the end of it – the amount might not be as high as Ezra was fearing. And if it were, they'd think of another solution that took everyone's needs into account.

My second story centres on Jenny and her teenage daughter Iris. Every year, Jenny, her partner, and Iris would go on a canal boat holiday with five other families. One year it had to be cancelled, which was a disappointment for them all, and one of the other mums, Alison, arranged a separate trip with three of the families in the group. This holiday didn't include Jenny. When Jenny found out about the substitute holiday, she felt extremely hurt that her family had been left out.

Things came to a head when Jenny and her family were on holiday in Cornwall later that year, in an area that happened to be two hours' drive from where Alison lived with her children. Iris (the daughter) was desperate to see her friends: 'Can we go, Mum, please? You can chat to Alison and we kids can go off on our own.' Jenny was torn. From her point of view, this would mean not only confronting her difficult feelings about Alison but also losing out on a day's canoeing on the river, which was something she'd been looking forward to for weeks. 'If Alison doesn't want to include me in her holiday then I don't want to see her either,' she muttered to herself. 'There's no way I'm giving up my canoeing for her.'

She was just about to explain to Iris that they couldn't go when Iris burst into tears. 'I really missed that canal trip and I'm worried we'll never go again. And I wasn't even invited on the other holiday. I don't know why they left me out!' Jenny immediately felt a rush of empathy with her daughter – of course she was upset. Why wouldn't she be? It didn't mean that Jenny's own needs weren't important anymore, but it gave her a new perspective.

The conversation then turned from being one in which they debated whether to see Alison or go canoeing, to one in which they came up with ideas about how everyone could enjoy themselves. In the sharing of feelings and needs, both Jenny and Iris started to move to a new place. Jenny's needs were for ease and enjoyment, with a strong fingerprint need for belonging, which was why she'd been triggered by her exclusion from the previous holiday. This, she realised, was a need she could take care of outside of the holiday – acknowledging it with self-empathy in the moment was enough for now.

'It sounds like you really want to see them,' Jenny said to Iris. 'I wonder if we can find a way to do it that suits us both?' After some discussion, it was decided that Jenny and her family would go canoeing during the day, and Alison and her family would come to join them in the evening.

Both of these stories show the power of sharing our vulnerability with people – it opens us up to a whole new way of thinking about a situation, in which needs rather than entrenched thinking predominate. It's also helpful, however, to see how the process works in different ways. In the first example, Annabel first identified with her need for health, and was then able to recognise Ezra's need for security. In the second one, Jenny first identified with Iris' need for connection, and this then freed her up to think about her own needs. There's no set order to whose needs you connect with first – the important factor is that you recognise both your needs and the other person's needs before looking for a strategy.

Isn't this another way of talking about compromise?

It's a fair question. On the surface, a compromise and a Needs Understanding solution can look much the same. However, they're arrived at by a completely different process, which is why they produce a better quality of outcome. In a compromise there's an inherent sense of conflict, in that either one party or both usually has to give up something that matters to them. A Needs Understanding strategy is a more abundant solution. It's a win-win way forward that also tends to be more imaginative and less two-dimensional than a compromise.

If we return to the story of Annabel with her heating, a compromise might have been to have the heating on half of the time. Annabel would have had to give up on the heating being on all day, and Ezra would have needed to reconcile himself with having less money for other things. Or they might have come up with the same solution as they actually did: a month's trial of full-time heating. In this case, Annabel would have got everything she wanted in the short term but with the worry that she might have to give it up after a month, and Ezra would have given up the peace of mind of having a low bill. But by going through the process of connecting with one another's needs, their strategy didn't *feel* like a compromise, it felt like a solution that worked equally for both of them. Ezra got to support Annabel's need for health, and Annabel got to contribute to his need for security. It was as if they were both standing alongside one another, rather than in opposite corners.

Holding onto needs and letting go of strategies

At the centre of Needs Understanding is a distinction between a strategy and a need. Our human needs are universal, but our strategies are not – they're the specific actions we take to meet our needs. For instance, we can all sometimes have the need for rest, but we can meet it in various ways: going to bed early, taking a nap, cutting back on alcohol, exercising, and other options. Different people might choose different strategies to meet the same need, depending on what works for them and what's possible at the time.

This matters because when we find ourselves in conflict with others, or even feeling distanced from those we want to be close to, it's the *strategies* that are getting in the way, not the needs that we're trying to meet. We sometimes need to view our strategies with a critical eye, especially if they don't seem to be solving problems for us in a constructive way.

Consider, for instance, Camille and Zarah. They're having an argument about what restaurant to go to, but that's not really what the disagreement is about. It might be that Camille has an underlying need to matter and have her voice heard, and that Zarah needs fun and respect. The strategy that each is using to meet her needs is to persuade the other woman over to her choice. So when Camille insists on her preferred place, she's imposing a strategy that doesn't meet Zarah's needs for fun and respect – probably quite the reverse. To find a way through this challenge, Camille can hold onto her own needs, but also be prepared to let go of her preferred strategy for meeting them.

A solution is most likely to work when you hold everyone's needs with care. One strategy for Camille might be to ask Zarah to come up with a solution that she thinks would work for them both. If Camille and Zarah are both familiar with Needs Understanding ideas, she could do this explicitly by identifying their needs. Camille could say something like, 'I guess my need is to matter, and I'm imagining you're looking for fun and maybe some respect? Can you suggest what would work for us both?' This is in itself respectful, which might help Zarah to relax and consider Camille's wishes more fully.

However, if only Camille has discovered Needs Understanding, or if identifying needs doesn't feel authentic or comfortable for either of them, she could try something like this: 'Zarah, I feel like we're getting stuck. I'd love for us to find something that works for us both. Do you have any ideas?' Without any mention of needs or strategies, Camille is inviting Zarah to think in terms of a jointly acceptable solution that takes care of them both.

A second option is for Camille to consider that her need to matter isn't one to put into the joint cooking pot, but one to take care of outside of their relationship. As she does this over time through recognising and empathising with it, it will stop 'running riot' subconsciously through her conversations with Zarah.

When both of them are thinking more along these lines, and less along the lines of 'I want to go to the restaurant I prefer,' there's likely to be more love and connection between them, even if one woman doesn't get her first choice. When we take care to understand everyone's needs, great strategies tend to follow.

Letting go of strategies can be easier said than done – some of them are so good for meeting our needs that we become attached to them, to the point at which we confuse them with the underlying needs that gave rise to them. This limits us. For a long while, I thought about moving to London from my home in Bristol because I knew it would help me to reach more people with my work. What held me back was my worry about my daughter having to change schools. 'I need to stay here because I can't move her halfway across the country, away from her friends and the school she loves,' I said to myself. What I was doing was to conflate my need to contribute to my daughter's wellbeing with my strategy, which was to stay in Bristol until she finished school.

After a visit to London together, I reassessed the situation. With my needs glasses on, I thought to myself, 'I really want her to be happy, and so far I've chosen to stay in Bristol because I believed it was the best way to make that happen. But maybe now she's older there are other possibilities that would look after both our needs, including my need for meaning in my work.' I realised that although my daughter would prefer to stay in Bristol and was nervous about moving, both of us could see real benefits in making the change to a school that was a better fit for her (alongside regular visits back to Bristol to keep in touch with friends). This helped me to lose my attachment to the strategy I'd been living with, and to see it for what it was – a solution I'd come up with that had passed its sell-by date. I allowed myself the possibility of seeing a different solution that could take care of all our needs, in a way that suited us both. In doing so, I held tightly to my needs, but lightly to my previous strategy.

When hidden fingerprint needs hold the key to solutions

John's an independent consultant and has been working with a business coach, who's pointed out that John can easily jump into the role of 'rescuer' for his clients. John regularly finds himself promising support to them that he can't deliver because he's so overloaded, which ends up with their feeling let down. For John, this drive to help people may betray a hidden fingerprint need for knowing that he's enough.

Toni has a pattern of unconsciously keeping her friends at arm's length until one of them has a problem. Then she leaps in to help, only to feel resentful if her friends aren't grateful.

She may have a fingerprint need for emotional safety, which she tries to meet by risking closeness with someone only when she thinks her efforts will be appreciated. Unfortunately, the opposite often happens.

If you were on the receiving end of John's fingerprint need for knowing he's enough, or Toni's fingerprint need for emotional safety, you might feel a bit confused, irritated, or disappointed. That's why it can be useful to have an awareness that other people have fingerprint needs. It helps you to make sense of otherwise baffling situations, to feel compassion for the other person, and to find ways forward that work for you both.

For instance, in the kind of situation we saw with John and Toni, there are two reactions we tend to have: saying we're grateful for the help when we don't really mean it, and cutting off the person helping us because it's so annoying. Both of these are likely to build a wall of disconnection. Instead, holding an awareness that their fingerprint needs might be at play, we can adopt a third position of maintaining compassion for them while still acting with care for our own needs. We might then replace avoidance and irritation with something like, 'I appreciate your offer to help and it means a lot that you've thought about me. But at the moment I'm okay on my own. I'll let you know if that changes.'

There's something to be aware of with this, though. When we have a sense of someone's fingerprint needs it can be tempting to feel a little superior. 'Oh, I know what's going on for her. She's just showing her fingerprint need for x.' It can be useful to have an attitude of humility here. Then, when we guess at someone's fingerprint needs, we're not trying to diagnose them or make a judgement. What we *are* doing is to help ourselves deal with a problematic scenario in a way that strengthens the relationship rather than blocking it.

PAUSE BOX

Use the framework with fingerprint needs

Have to hand: the list of needs.

As you become more familiar with your fingerprint needs, it becomes easier to recognise when someone else is caught up in their own.

Think of a recurring situation, or one in which you've been triggered into a sudden, powerful emotion. It doesn't matter whether or not it involves someone else – go for one that prompts you to want to understand more about your reaction, or one where you'd like to find a different solution.

Take the list of needs and walk through the Needs Understanding framework, as described earlier in this chapter.

Do you notice any needs that might be fingerprint needs? What light (if any) does connecting with your needs shed on the situation?

If you get stuck, you may find it helpful to go back to Chapter 4 (What makes you tick?) and use it to help you discover your needs.

Using the framework with internal dilemmas

So often, when we're faced with a decision, we have an internal conflict about what to do. Different parts of us want outcomes that seem irreconcilable, and we can end up bypassing the needs and 'trying on' various strategies, with the result that we go around in mental circles.

There's another way to approach internal dilemmas, which is to think about them through the lens of needs. The Needs Understanding process of resolving an internal dilemma is much the same as when we have a conflict with other people, but now the argument is with ourselves rather than someone else. We can still use the same basic framework to listen to the different parts of ourselves that want different things, and to connect with the needs behind them. Once we have all the needs in the pot, we look for a way through the problem that works better for us.

When we have an internal dilemma, it can sometimes be tricky to see it clearly, and more uncomfortable to listen to all the conflicting elements. Let's take the case of Leroy, who wants to propose an exciting and transformational idea to his boss Katrina. He's convinced that it has potential, but he also knows that Katrina can be dismissive of new concepts. Should he go for it or not?

Mulling over the problem during the weekend, Leroy can spot two inner voices. One says, 'This is an amazing idea! It may be a brave move, but the thought of proposing it makes me feel excited.' When he asks himself what's so important to him about the idea, he finds himself realising that he's been feeling bored at work for some time. 'I want to feel alive and challenged! Those are the needs I'm trying to take care of.'

The second voice is harder for him to hear, because he doesn't like what it says: 'I'm scared of feeling embarrassed and small. She might throw my idea back in my face.' Leroy can ignore that voice ('It's all fine, really'), he can judge himself for it ('I shouldn't be feeling like this – it's no big deal'), or he can rationalise it ('I'll never have such a great opportunity again

– I should just go for it'). However, he knows that when he pushes certain parts of himself away instead of listening to them, they only shout more loudly to attract his attention to the needs behind them. Until he hears their message, they end up running the show, getting in the way of his dreams and ambitions. So instead of avoiding the second voice, Leroy does his best to listen to it with empathy and hear the needs behind it. 'It's understandable that I'm feeling like this. My idea is important to me, and I'm afraid of rejection from Katrina. I really want to be heard.'

Once he feels more at peace with his needs for aliveness, challenge, and to be heard, it also occurs to him to think about the needs that Katrina might have, most specifically for respect. If he goes to her with an idea that appears half-baked, she might feel impatient or angry because her need isn't being taken care of.

Now that all the needs are in the pot, Leroy's able to think more clearly about how he can find a way through the situation that would work for both him and Katrina. What can he do to show respect for her in how he presents his idea? He instantly realises that he hasn't done enough groundwork in terms of costing it out and analysing the pros and cons – it seems obvious now. This is the sort of evidence that Katrina will need if she's to take him seriously. So he creates a full proposal, ready to take to Katrina on Monday.

If you only take one thing from this chapter...

- When we find ourselves in difficult relationships or struggling with intractable problems, it's often because we've jumped straight from situation to strategy without considering the underlying needs at play.

And if you take a few more...

- To hold everyone's needs with care, we first need to empathise with ourselves and with the other person, so that we become aware of all the needs at play.

- Once we've identified the needs as best we can, we can generate more creative and constructive strategies than if we hadn't paid attention to them.

- When we confuse needs and strategies, we become entrenched in positions which don't work for us; it helps if we hold tightly to our needs, but lightly to our strategies.

- A compromise and a Needs Understanding solution are different, in that a compromise feels as if one or both parties have given something up, while a Needs Understanding solution feels as though everyone has won.

- When we have an internal dilemma, paying attention to the uncomfortable voices and the needs underneath can help us find a happier way forward.

Chapter 9

Beyond right and wrong

Moving from opposition to collaboration

Declan and Lizzie had been living together for a year and were very happy with one another… with one major exception. Declan was being driven mad by Lizzie's clutter and mess. While he would come home from work, hang up his coat, and put his shoes in the closet, Lizzie would throw her coat onto the sofa and kick off her boots as soon as she walked through the door.

It wasn't only the coats and shoes. When Lizzie cooked a meal, the kitchen ended up in a complete state; when she got ready to go out for the evening, their bedroom floor was left carpeted with clothes; and when she worked from home, she'd leave a trail of papers from her office to the living room. If Declan remonstrated about the mess, she'd look surprised. From her point of view, there wasn't a problem – it was only a few bits and pieces here and there. Why couldn't he work around them?

Declan was torn. On the one hand, some of Lizzie's most lovable qualities were her spontaneity and sense of fun, and he could see that they went hand in hand with her messiness.

He cherished the happy times they had together and would never want that to change. But on the other hand, he found it stressful and annoying to be living in what felt to him like a rubbish dump.

He tried asking Lizzie if she'd clear up after herself; this would work once, but she'd forget the next time. He tried putting up with the mess, but he only ended up exploding with anger when it became too much for him. He even tried tidying it up himself, but the faster he did it, the quicker her belongings seemed to fill the space. Their days were punctuated by arguments, and then he'd feel guilty because he wanted her to be happy and for them to get along. The constant see-sawing of frustration and guilt was exhausting for him.

Finally, he realised that if they were to resolve this issue he'd have to regain a sense of connection with Lizzie. His first step, however, was to consider the problem from his own point of view; if he didn't do this, he wouldn't be able to create the emotional space to understand what was going on for her. His perspective was that there was stuff lying all over the house, and that he didn't function well in mess. 'It's understandable that you're so annoyed with it,' he told himself. 'You hate living like this and it gets in the way of you enjoying your home. You're not a bad person for feeling this way – it's okay to ask for what you want.' As he empathised with himself and his annoyance, he gained a sense of his own need for peace of mind. Now he felt ready to explore what was going on for Lizzie, and to see the situation as a shared problem that they could work on together.

What might her perspective on it be, he thought? Declan recognised that to Lizzie there was no issue with the untidiness itself – in fact, she enjoyed the ease and freedom of leaving her stuff wherever it fell. And yet he could see that the mess still created a problem for her as well, in that it resulted in his being angry with her, and she didn't enjoy being blamed or shouted at. She wanted connection and harmony just as much as he did. Now he could start to look for a way forward with her, and he began by voicing what he imagined might be up for both of them.

'I can see that for you it's easy to leave your things lying around, and I want you to feel free to do that. At the same time, for me, it's different. I get annoyed when there's mess all over the house because I need a clear space to function well. And neither of us likes me losing my temper about it. Any ideas about how we could look after both of us with this?'

Lizzie was touched by Declan's efforts to describe the problem from her point of view, and committed to finding a solution that could work for both of them. The conversation carried on in various forms for several weeks, until a breakthrough was achieved when Lizzie came up with an idea. She'd have one room in the house (her home office) that she could leave in a mess, and would try not to clutter up the rest of the space. If sometimes she were to forget, Declan would try to remind her without becoming angry, and if she weren't around, he'd put Lizzie's belongings in her office himself. It's an arrangement that's working well to this day.

While you may not have been through exactly the same challenge, you might remember times when you've faced something similar. It could be an annoying colleague, a misbehaving child, or a wider problem such as frustration with the political climate or despair at the state of the environment. The question is always: what can I do?

The answer, which we'll explore in this chapter, centres on seeing ourselves as being in *partnership* with others rather than in opposition. It opens up an array of fresh possibilities for solving problems both in our own lives and in the world at large. We can do this without harming our relationships; in fact, the nurturing of our connections with others is built into the process.

The opposition paradigm

When we find ourselves in disagreement with someone, it's as if we're engaged in a power struggle. The problem we face is like a mountain sitting between us, with each party trying to find a way to remove it. If we leap into solving the problem through our preferred strategies without considering the needs behind them, we'll be pulling in different directions and the mountain will stay stubbornly where it is.

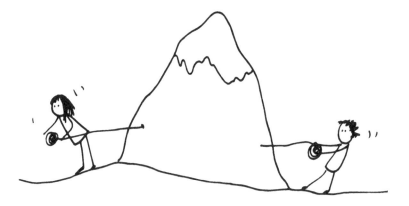

Standing on either side of the mountain as lonely figures, we can't see one another – we lose our mutual connection. Because we're looking at the problem from opposing positions, we can only see our side of things, rather than appreciating the other person's perspective. We wish the problem would go away, but only on the condition that our own needs are met, irrespective of theirs. And we're scared that if we let go of our strategy to solve the problem, we also have to abandon any hope of meeting our needs. This is the opposition paradigm.

Our mindset when we're in opposition to someone:

- It's my problem or it's your problem.

- The problem sits between you and me, blocking our connection.

- I can't see you – I can only see the problem.

- My way is the right way.

- I'm not letting go of my way, whatever you say or do.

- One of us has to win and one of us has to lose.

- Conflict is bad and must be avoided.

This oppositional thinking applies more widely than just to our personal or work relationships; it underpins every aspect of our lives. Our social structures – families, classrooms, workplaces, and public institutions – are usually based on a hierarchical system of control and privilege. Those at the top have rights and freedoms that those at the bottom are denied. And the latter group – for instance children, the low paid, and marginal groups – live with the fear of reprisal from those above. From early on, many of us absorb the message that we're in competition with other people, whether it be with our siblings for parental attention, other children at school for exam grades, or as adults for jobs and financial rewards. No wonder we place ourselves in opposition to people when we disagree with them; it seems as if it's our only option if we're to survive in this society of winners and losers.

If you're wondering whether the opposition paradigm is actually that prevalent, the next time you're out and about – on a bus or in a shop – it can be interesting to listen to the conversations around you. What you might find is that our normal way of socialising is to have an 'enemy' against whom we can define ourselves, whether it be a politician we didn't vote for, our children who don't behave the way we'd like, our partner who enrages us, or our colleagues who let us down. It often seems that we share our world with people whom we find challenging, incomprehensible, or unpleasant – sometimes even scary. Some of those people are strangers we never need to meet, and others are family members, colleagues, or acquaintances. If we don't know how to engage with them with understanding and respect but without giving up on our own values, we end up either in conflict or retreating into our personal social bubbles. This means that we're not able to influence their views. On a micro level it can lead to disagreements within families, and on a macro level it sits behind conflict between communities and nations.

Equally, we can align ourselves with those we see as similar to us, such as people who share our background or have a familiar world view. Spending time with people who seem to be the most like us is often a helpful way to meet important needs such as safety, belonging, comfort and ease. However, the problem can come when they're our whole world.

There's an alternative. The tools we've explored in the Needs Understanding approach encourage a shift towards a *partnership* paradigm instead of an oppositional one. In this, we hold all needs with equal care so that more of them are met for everyone – the assumption being that it makes sense to find solutions that work for all parties. We step out of the thinking that those with different opinions are on the other side of the mountain, and step into the thinking that everyone is on the same side, facing the problem together.

The partnership paradigm

In the partnership paradigm, you set the intention of finding a solution that meets everyone's needs. That involves being ready to let go of the strategy you've set your heart on, while still holding tightly to your own needs.

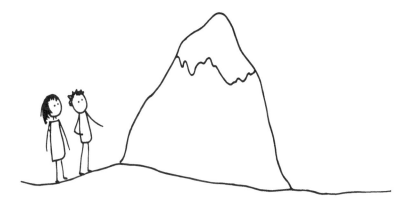

The key point here is that you're not seeing the other person as wrong, but as having views you don't like – views that *don't meet your needs*. Instead of fighting about which strategy to use, you try to understand their needs (and your own), with a view to finding a way forward that works for you both. In doing so you also build a closer connection with the person. And, like the rest of Needs Understanding, you can do this alone – you don't need them to have learned about it or to apply its thinking. It can work just as well if the new approach comes only from you.

Our mindset when we've shifted to a partnership paradigm:

- It's our problem – we're on the same team, working to solve the problem.

- I've moved around to stand by your side – I can see you without blame, and our connection is back.

- It doesn't take the problem away, but let's deal with it together.

- My way might not be the only way.

- It's important that I don't let go of my needs, but I'll do my best to let go of my preferred strategy. And I'll definitely listen to your needs and try to hold them with equal care.

- Everyone can win.

- Conflict is an opportunity for us to find a better solution.

The partnership paradigm enables us to move away from thinking only in terms of our own preferred strategies, and towards an understanding of the needs at play – which are universal. This builds connection, so that an answer that doesn't work for both parties doesn't seem to make sense anymore.

Just as the opposition paradigm underpins how we see ourselves as a society, the partnership paradigm also has benefits that go well beyond our individual relationships. Imagine a girl is sent to the head teacher's office for disrupting her class. Instead of reprimanding her for 'bad' behaviour, the head talks with her about what needs she was trying to meet when she acted as she did. He supports her to find ways of satisfying those needs that work as well for her teacher and classmates as for herself.

Or picture a shift in how we organise our political system. Instead of an adversarial one in which politicians argue about who's right and wrong, imagine a set-up in which leaders focus on needs. They listen and try to understand one another, rather than scoring political points. Proposed legislation is evaluated against the needs that it will or won't meet, and the common challenge is to pass laws that will best take care of the needs of all citizens.

In each of these examples, no one has to give up on the clarity of their beliefs or to silence the strength of their feelings, and space is freed up to explore a range of creative solutions.

Ideas for what to say in the partnership paradigm

Because we're so used to speaking in oppositional terms ('I can't believe they did that!' or 'Why does she always get her own way?'), it can feel as if we're exploring new territory when we want to adopt a partnership approach. One option is to think about the kind of language that reflects it, so I've offered some examples below. As ever, being authentic is always the most important thing, so if they don't sound like you, feel free to use them as an illustration to help you come up with something better. Also, the energy behind your words is more important than the ones you choose to use. When you're genuinely able to see the problem as a shared one, your body language, tone of voice, and gestures will do much of the job for you.

'I hear that you're frustrated, and at the same time I'm upset. Do you have any suggestions for how we can approach this so it works for both of us?'

'So we have a problem here! What can we do?'

'I don't agree with what you're suggesting, and I'd like to understand more about why you think that's the best solution?'

'I've noticed there have been quite a few times when I've felt annoyed in relation to you, and it may be the same the other way round. I'd love to have a conversation so we can find a way forward that works for us both. Would that be helpful? When's the best time?'

Respectful boundaries – saying 'no' with care

There will be times when you can't find a way forward that works for everyone, and in these cases you may want to consider your options. You could agree to a solution that doesn't meet your needs, leaving you feeling resentful. You could force through a solution that doesn't meet the other person's needs, leaving them feeling upset. Or you could stay stuck in the belief that your happiness is dependent on them shifting their behaviour, and keep trying to make them change. None of those tend to work well, especially in the longer term. However, what you can also do is to set a boundary. Effectively, you say 'no'.

Even when it's necessary to set a boundary, you may still want to keep as much connection as possible between yourself and others. An important factor in achieving this is your consideration for the other person's views and the needs behind them. Needs Understanding offers an approach to setting boundaries that's respectful, and still holds everyone's needs with care. When you set a respectful boundary, you:

- take care of your needs and values, but without trying to change the other person's;

- are not trying to teach anyone else a lesson;

- aren't setting the boundary to penalise someone.

It's the difference between saying, 'I'm not phoning you this evening – you need to stop being so demanding,' and 'I need to rest this evening and won't be calling you. I'll ring you tomorrow.' In the former you put the other person in the wrong, but in the latter you explain your boundary in terms of your needs, so there's less risk of them hearing it as an attack (even if they may be disappointed). You're taking responsibility for your needs and owning the boundary, rather than trying to make them change their mind or encourage them to see themselves as being at fault.

There will be times when setting a boundary from the start is the safest and most caring thing you can do, even if you don't have the time or inner resources to set a respectful one. This is especially the case if there's a risk to your physical or emotional safety. A clear example is that of a woman who's been emotionally abused by her partner over many months, and who leaves the situation without engaging with him. To try to do so could risk further harm to her wellbeing.

A more day-to-day scenario might be when you pull your child from a busy road without negotiation or explanation; there'll be time to empathise with shocked or angry tears afterwards. Or you're exhausted and running on empty, and to avoid yelling at your spouse you say, 'I need to get out of the room now to calm down – I'll talk later!' When you're feeling more resourced, and if you want to rebuild the connection that was lost when you set a boundary this way, you can return to the conversation using your listening and empathising tools.

Ideas for what to say when you set a boundary

Once again, it's less about the particular words you use, and more about the energy and intention behind them. In a partnership approach, boundary-setting involves being aware of all the needs at play. However, because you aren't able to see a way to meet both parties' needs in this situation, you're saying 'no' in order to protect your own. In the following examples, many of the words could be said with either a punitive or a protective energy; it's a protective energy that enables you to set the boundary with respect.

When you're protecting your need for peace of mind: *'I want to feel confident that you're safe when you walk to school on your own. You can do it when you're ten, but not before.'*

When you're protecting your value of care for the environment: *'I'd love to come to your birthday weekend in Budapest, and at the same time it's important to me to cut back on my air miles to help the environment. I'm so sorry, but I won't be part of the gang this time.'*

When you're protecting your need for rest: *'Sadly no – I'd love to support you, and it doesn't feel doable at the moment, given how tired I am.'*

Thinking back to Declan and Lizzie, let's imagine that they weren't able to reach an agreement about whether or not Lizzie would start tidying up. What if she refused to discuss it, and Declan still wanted to have a loving relationship with her while also protecting his need for peace of mind? There are some things that he has the power to change, and there are some that he doesn't. He could try to put pressure on her with a guilt trip or manipulation. That may or may not succeed, but it would almost certainly be at some cost to their relationship. He could decide that he would live with the mess. That might be a way forward if he'd exhausted all his other options, but only if he genuinely felt that – because he valued so many other things about his relationship with Lizzie – he was able to live with his needs unmet. Otherwise he'd be more likely to feel resentment, which he'd take out on Lizzie in other ways.

Declan can also set a boundary. He can say something like this to Lizzie: 'I really need clear space to function well, and I can't see a way of letting go of that and still being okay within myself. I know you don't want to talk about it, so I'm going to pick up your things and put them in your office. I know this isn't what you want.'

PAUSE BOX

Why is it so hard to say 'no'?

There are a number of reasons why we may find it hard to say 'no', including:

- thinking that our needs don't matter;

- assuming that people won't like us;

- avoiding conflicts;

- not knowing how to say 'no';

- having had our 'no' ignored by others in the past; and

- being socially conditioned to say 'yes'.

Reflect on times when you've said 'yes' but wish you'd said 'no'. What made you say 'yes'? Would you like to say 'no' next time? What do you need to do to make that possible?

Connecting across divides

There's nothing wrong with disagreement. On the contrary, it not only reveals that there may be multiple solutions to a problem, but it also increases the chances of finding one that meets more needs for more people. The world needs differing perspectives in order to benefit from the wide range of views that humans are gifted with. The problem is not with disagreement, but with disconnection.

When we disconnect from ourselves and our needs, and from the needs of people who see the world differently from us, we create polarisation. We entrench ourselves in our world views because we don't know how to engage with people without giving up what's so important to us. That leads us to feel angry and frustrated with one another, which isn't a helpful position to be in to create happiness in our lives or to make the world a better place.

What Needs Understanding offers us is a way of disagreeing powerfully with someone without making them 'wrong'. It can be a difficult idea to put into practice at first. We may worry that if we understand *why* someone thinks the polar opposite to us, we have to accept their point of view. That's not necessarily the case. Instead, the option is there to stop seeing them as the enemy or the 'other side', and to start to make sense of what's going on for them. What needs do they have that make them adopt a view that we find so unpalatable? When we look at the disagreement through the lens of needs, the conversation moves from making the other party wrong and ourselves right, to looking at how the strategies that each has chosen aren't meeting everyone's needs. Through this lens we can find ways forward that work for everyone, while staying in connection and partnership with one another.

If you only take one thing from this chapter...

- In the partnership paradigm, we stop seeing those with different views as wrong, and instead look for the needs they're trying to meet.

And if you take a few more...

- When we're in an oppositional struggle, it's as if we have a mountain between us and the other person, with each of us clinging to our own strategy as a way of solving the disagreement.

- In the partnership paradigm, we move to the same side of the mountain; we build and maintain connection with one another, as well as finding a mutually acceptable way forward.

- Partnership problem-solving sees behaviour we disagree with not as wrong, but as not meeting our needs.

- In the partnership paradigm, we hold tightly to our needs but are also ready to let go of our strategies for meeting them.

- If we can't resolve an issue through a partnership approach, we can choose to set a respectful boundary; this protects our needs while still taking care of our relationship with the other person.

Conclusion

Choosing connection in a competitive world

The four skill areas of Needs Understanding can offer us a huge amount. When we **listen with empathy**, we enable someone to feel heard and understood – that alone can be transformational. But more than that, we can tap into what that person might be needing, so that we can stand alongside them rather than in opposition. When we **understand our needs with compassion**, we're able to make sense of ourselves and the situations we find difficult, so we can navigate them with an ease that would never have felt possible before. When we **speak to be heard**, we create constructive conversations that put across our own important thoughts, but also build a safe space for the other person's needs to be considered. And when we **act with care for everyone's needs**, we find paths through problems that take account of everyone involved; solutions appear that were previously hidden to us, and we come out of challenging situations with our relationships intact or even strengthened.

There are so many transformational outcomes available to us when we look at the world through the lens of needs that it can be hard to know where to start – and of course, it depends on your priorities and what you want to change. If your aim is to have closer and more harmonious relationships with your loved ones, you can use Needs Understanding as a practical set of tools for achieving them. If your ambition is to transform your workplace or your industry, you'll see problem-solving and relationship-building in a completely new light. And if you long for all of that and more – to influence whole groups of people to work together to overcome seemingly insurmountable problems – it gives you a fresh perspective on creating a constructive and engaging way of behaving that has the potential to move mountains.

When I refer to having an impact on a larger scale, it can make the notion of personal empowerment seem small – and it's anything but. If each of us were to see other people's behaviour through the lens of needs, and if we truly believed that we were all acting in an attempt to meet our needs, the world would be a different place. We'd see those on the other side of the political and social divide as potential collaborators; we'd communicate more easily with people from different backgrounds; and as parents and educators we'd raise young people to be empowered in their lives, so that they in turn can make a difference.

The beauty of Needs Understanding is partly in its flexibility. You can see it at a purely practical level and use it to easily fix problems that would previously have been difficult. Or you can engage with it at a deeper emotional level, gradually shifting your thinking to the point where it doesn't make sense to do things the old way anymore.

It's one simple concept that ripples through every area of life. It frees you up to recognise your own potential as a creative problem solver, who can bring their insights and empathy into the most challenging of situations. There's an immense personal strength that comes from valuing your needs and asserting them, while at the same time considering those of others with equal care.

However, regardless of how much you might want to take advantage of what's on offer, it can feel overwhelming to think about how you're going to make it work in your life. When something is new, it doesn't always come naturally at first. It's a bit like learning to drive all over again. Instead of turning on the engine, checking your mirrors, and moving off without thinking about it, you're concentrating on every single action *and* keeping your eyes on the road.

There are a couple of things you could try as a way of making it simpler for yourself. The first is to take a look back at the four skill areas of Needs Understanding and ask yourself which, if you could get just a bit better at it, would have the biggest impact on your experience of life. You can then choose to focus on that. A second way might be to revisit the Pause Boxes that are dotted throughout the book, working through one in depth each day or week. You can find a list of Pause Boxes with their page numbers at the end of the book.

Once you've seen and understood the principles of Needs Understanding, you may find yourself looking at life in a new way. Whenever you feel stuck or confused, you'll know that there's a way to make life easier and more meaningful, and a powerful set of tools to bring you closer to people. The old, habitual outlook won't seem to work as well anymore, and will start to give way to a more beautiful and timeless understanding that is yours for the taking. The Needs Understanding approach is one step towards a society in which empathy and understanding are deeply embedded. It's a world where our common experience of life is not one of aloneness, struggle, or apathy, but of community, meaning, and shared joy. Join me there?

Afterword

Needs and the natural world

When I thought about what to say in this book, I decided – after some struggle – to explain how Needs Understanding works only from a human perspective. That's because I think it's the simplest way to learn it, and my aim is for you to grasp the concepts as easily as possible. But there are other needs to consider in this world as well, which are animal and environmental needs.

The principles are the same: just like humans, plants and animals have needs of their own. Whatever we do, we can choose to take into account the natural world and its inhabitants, or we can ignore or minimise them. In recent history, many of us have seen our planet from a human-centric perspective, with us meeting our own needs to the detriment of other living beings. At the moment, the risk is that we tumble even further down this path and with potentially disastrous consequences.

However, just as Needs Understanding can transform the quality of our human connections, so it can be applied to the wider world. When we use our awareness of needs to act with care for every form of life, or to look for creative solutions that take care of all the needs in the world, we're embracing Needs Understanding in its most inclusive form.

Appendix
Useful LISTS

List of needs

This list appears on pages 2–3. You can download a 'print out and keep' copy at www.needs-understanding.com.

Physical Needs
Air
Food
Health
Light
Movement
Rest
Shelter
Touch
Water

Security
Emotional safety
Peace of mind
Physical safety
Protection
Stability

Freedom
Autonomy
Choice
Ease
Independence
Responsibility
Space

To Matter
Acceptance
Acknowledgement
Care
Compassion
Consideration
Empathy
Recognition
Respect
To be heard
To be seen
Trust
Understanding

Play / Leisure
Fun
Humour
Joy
Pleasure
Rejuvenation
Relaxation

Understanding
Awareness
Clarity

Discovery
Learning
Stimulation

Connection
Affection
Appreciation
Attention
Closeness
Companionship
Contact
Harmony
Intimacy
Love
Nurture
Sexual expression
Tenderness
Warmth

Community
Belonging
Communication
Cooperation
Equality
Inclusion
Mutuality
Participation
Partnership
Self-expression
Sharing
Support
Tolerance

Sense of Self
Agency
Authenticity

Competence
Dignity
Effectiveness
Empowerment
Growth
Healing
Honesty
Integrity
Knowing I'm enough
Mattering to myself
Self-acceptance
Self-care
Self-realisation

Meaning
Aliveness
Challenge
Consciousness
Contribution
Creativity
Exploration
Integration
Purpose

Transcendence
Beauty
Celebration
Communion
Faith
Flow
Hope
Inspiration
Mourning
Mystery
Peace
Presence

List of feelings

This list is inspired by the work of Marianne Göthlin: www.skolande.se. It appears on pages 65–66. You can download a 'print out and keep' copy at www.needs-understanding.com.

Glad, happy, hopeful, joyful, satisfied, delighted, blissful, courageous, grateful, confident, relieved, touched, proud, optimistic, overjoyed, warm, wonderful.

Excited, amazed, amused, exuberant, astonished, breathless, eager, energetic, enthusiastic, fascinated, inspired, interested, intrigued, stimulated.

Peaceful, calm, content, expansive, blissful, satisfied, relaxed, secure, clear, comfortable, pleasant, relieved.

Loving, warm, affectionate, tender, friendly, sensitive, compassionate, nurtured, trusting, helpful, moved.

Playful, energetic, refreshed, alert, stimulated, exuberant, adventurous, eager, enthusiastic, curious.

Rested, relaxed, alert, refreshed, strong, alive, energised.

Thankful, grateful, appreciative, fulfilled.

Sad, lonely, heavy, helpless, grieving, overwhelmed, distant, discouraged, distressed, dismayed, concerned, depressed, despairing, disappointed.

Yearning, longing, nostalgic, remorseful, pining, aching, regretful, wistful.

Scared, afraid, fearful, terrified, nervous, panicky, horrified, anxious, lonely, sceptical, suspicious, alarmed, apprehensive, frightened, jealous, surprised.

Angry, aggravated, frustrated, furious, mad, enraged, hostile, pessimistic, resentful, disgusted, annoyed, disappointed, displeased, upset.

Confused, hesitant, troubled, torn, uneasy, worried, apprehensive, bewildered, disturbed, reluctant, insecure.

Tired, exhausted, indifferent, overwhelmed, burnt out, helpless, heavy, sleepy, withdrawn, apathetic, bored, lazy, numb.

Uncomfortable, pained, uneasy, hurt, miserable, embarrassed, ashamed, guilty, impatient, irritated, restless.

List of physical sensations

This list only appears on this page. You can download a 'print out and keep' copy at www.needs-understanding.com.

Warm
Flowing
Fluid
Glowing
Light
Melting
Open
Expansive
Radiating
Relaxed
Releasing
Full

Spacious
Airy
Calm
Expanded
Floating
Still

Tender
Achy
Bruised
Raw
Sensitive
Sore
Itchy
Prickly

Fluttery
Bubbly
Buzzy
Breathless
Energised
Rushing
Streaming
Tingling

Burning
Cutting
Hot
Piercing
Sharp
Throbbing
Pounding

Shaky
Dizzy
Nauseous
Nervy
Queasy
Shivery
Sweaty
Trembling
Twitchy
Wobbly

Numb
Cold
Cool
Frozen
Icy
Cut off
Blocked
Disconnected
Stuck
Wooden

Tense
Clenched
Closed
Congested
Constricted
Contracted
Tight
Knotted

Hollow
Drained
Empty
Heavy
Dense
Dull

List of false feelings

This list appears on page 114. You can download a 'print out and keep' copy at www.needs-understanding.com.

Abandoned	Insulted	Ripped off
Abused	Intimidated	Rushed
Attacked	Invalidated	Shunned
Belittled	Judged	Smothered
Betrayed	Left out	Suffocated
Blamed	Let down	Taken for granted
Boxed in	Manipulated	Trampled
Bullied	Misunderstood	Unappreciated
Cheated	Neglected	Unheard
Coerced	Overlooked	Unloved
Criticised	Overpowered	Unsupported
Diminished	Patronised	Used
Discounted	Pressured	Victimised
Hassled	Put down	Wronged
Ignored	Rejected	

The author

About Alice

Alice Sheldon is the creator of Needs Understanding, a fresh and exciting approach for finding practical solutions to problems, and building relationships that work.

Alice graduated from Oxford University with an MA in Psychology and Neurophysiology. She's always had a strong interest in how we can contribute to the creation of a more inclusive world. This has taken her on a career path that includes being a secondary school teacher, a barrister, and leading the Bar's national pro bono charity, Advocate.

During this time Alice came across two life-changing pieces of understanding. The first was psychotherapy, which inspired a deep learning journey. The second was Nonviolent Communication (NVC), which led to her becoming a Certified Trainer with the Center for Nonviolent Communication.

Subsequently, she developed a model of partnership parenting, and for a decade worked with hundreds of fellow parents, helping them to create thriving relationships with their children. This became the springboard for her creation of Needs Understanding, which brings a partnership approach into all spheres of life.

Alice shares Needs Understanding globally with individuals and organisations. Like what you've read? Find out how to take it further at www.needs-understanding.com.

On the shoulders of giants

Ideas that have contributed to Needs Understanding

Each of us builds on the work of those who've come before, absorbing what they've created and applying it to help us make sense of our own experience in the world. I long to recognise the work of all of those whose ideas have gone into my creation of Needs Understanding. In the writing of this book, I made the choice not to attribute specific ideas either to myself or to others in the main body of the text. This was partly because I didn't want to break the flow, and partly because many of the ideas come from a multitude of sources. So this section is a place to recognise and thank those who've directly influenced the development of the ideas in Needs Understanding. Including the names of certain individuals feels important, and yet it isn't intended to be an exhaustive list.

The centrality of needs is an idea that's inspired by the work of Marshall Rosenberg, creator of Nonviolent Communication (NVC). I'm so grateful for his legacy, and throughout Needs Understanding his influence is very significant. To name some of the ideas that I first discovered from him: actions as an attempt to meet needs; the 'yes' behind the 'no'; distinguishing feelings from false feelings; understanding judgemental thoughts as an expression of needs; the needs at play in regret; the distinction between needs and strategies.

Cheryl Garner was my psychotherapist for many years, and it is largely through our work together that my understanding of empathy and self-empathy evolved to where it is today. The ideas which have come from her are harder for me to list individually because they're integrated so deeply into how I work with Needs Understanding. Her compassion, warmth, and courage have influenced me in countless ways.

Gina Lawrie and Bridget Belgrave taught me NVC at the beginning. The cards approach to the Needs Understanding framework is directly inspired by a process that Gina and Bridget developed called the NVC Dance Floors. I've found it to be a powerful aid to learning.

The neuroscience has come from a range of sources, perhaps most notably Daniel Siegel. I've learned much from Alfie Kohn's extensive work on the adverse effects of praise and reward in education and parenting. Harville Hendrix and Helen LaKelly Hunt created Imago Relationship Therapy, which encourages compassionate understanding and acceptance of each other through listening, validation, and empathy. They use islands as a metaphor in relationships, and one of their books (below) is my favourite nonfiction book of all time. Kirsten Kristensen's clarity, wisdom, and warmth helped me to develop my ideas of how NVC and psychotherapy fit together. Miki Kashtan has been an important mentor in a whole range of areas, and particularly in relation to putting needs consciousness into action in the world.

Over the years I've lived and shared Needs Understanding with many. It's those friends, colleagues, and students who've shown me more than anyone how to put everything together so that it's clear and learnable and can be easily applied. Needs Understanding isn't meant to be a static model, and I look forward to evolving it in collaboration over many years to come.

How to find those I've named:

Alfie Kohn: Kohn, A. (2017). *Punished by Rewards: The Trouble with Gold Stars, Incentive Plans, A's, Praise, and Other Bribes.* Boston: Houghton Mifflin Co.

Cheryl Garner: www.psychotherapy.org.uk/therapist/cheryl-garner

Daniel Siegel: www.drdansiegel.com

Gina Lawrie and Bridget Belgrave: www.NvcDanceFloors.com

Harville Hendrix and Helen LaKelly Hunt (2019). *Getting the Love You Want: A Guide for Couples.* Third Edition (Reprint, Revised, Updated ed.). St Martin's Griffin.

Kirsten Kristensen: www.kommunikationforlivet.dk

Marshall Rosenberg (2015). *Nonviolent Communication: A Language of Life* (3rd ed.). Encinitas, CA: PuddleDancer Press.

Miki Kashtan: www.mikikashtan.org

Book Friends

At an early stage of writing, I started the Book Friends, a group of friends from near and far who have supported me on the book's journey. It's been invaluable to have your advice and encouragement, and I love the community we've built together. Thank you to every one of you for being part of the team that has brought this book into being.

The Book Friends at the point of going to press are:

Abi Spence
Alanah Larielle
Alessandra Perrone
Alexander Brandon
Alice Tuppen-Corps
Alison Hayman
Alison Jones
Alyson Wills
Amy Whitworth
Anna Butler-Whittaker
Anna March
Annett Zupke
Åse Thorsén
Barry Allsop
Becky Hall
Bonnie Williams
Caroline Silver
Cath Hubbuck
Catherine Weetman

Cathy Swift
Catriona Oliphant
Christelle Brindel
Christine Schulz
Claire Honor
Cleona Lira
Corrie Bell
Dawn Ellis
Debbie Redfern
Di White
Diane Lester
Dorota Godby
Dorothy Martin
Dorothy Nesbit
Emily Allsop
Emma Bairstow-Ellis
Emma Crane
Fi Macmillan
Fiona Buckle

Fiona Macbeth
Francesca (Froo) Signore
Gabriele Grunt
Gemma Box
Ginny Carter
Heather Monro
Helen Beedham
Helen Downhill
Helen O'Grady
Isobel Ripley
Jacqueline Mitton
Jenna Self
Jo McHale
Jo Raeburn
John Odell
Jonathan Silver
Josephine McCourt
Judith Payne
Justyna Sokolowska
Katie McMahon
Katie Player
Ken Dickson
Kim Young
Kirsten Rose
Kirsty Leggate
Krista Powell Edwards
Lara Montgomery
Laura Harvey
Lel Pender
Lily Horseman
Lis O'Kelly
Lisa Beasley
Liv Bargman
Louise Wiles
Lucy Ryan

Mandy Carr
Marcella Chan
Marianna Asimenou
Marianne Fennema
Marieke van Soest
Mark Hutchison
Mark Pilkington
Matt Wait
Mona Jeffreys
Monique Roffey
Myriam Melot
Natasha Broke
Niki Matyjasik
Oliver Cain
Paul Snell
Paula Ellen
Pavli Minns
Penny Spawforth
Peter Sim
Rachel Garstang
Rachel Hudson
Rachel Palmer
Rebecca Crossthwaite
Refkah A'Court-Mond
Rhona Donaldson
Robert Gill
Roz Adams
Russ Ayres
Ruth Patchett
Sam Brightwell
Samaśuri Howes
Sarah Davison
Sarah Heydon
Sarah Hulme
Sarah Mook

Sheila Greer
Sophie Docker
Sue Johnston
Susie Self
Suz Paul
Suzy Andricopoulos
Tamara Laporte
Tanya Forgan
Teresa McDonell

Tom Wilkinson
Tracy Argent
Tracy Seed
Ulli Nykvist
Veronica Munro
Violaine Felten
Yolande Anastasi
Yvonne Wiley

Acknowledgements

When I wrote the first draft of *Why Weren't We Taught This at School?*, the feedback was unanimous: 'Alice, it's unreadable!' It's only because I have been surrounded throughout by the most wonderful team that I have been able to create my ideal book.

Ginny Carter brought her consummate writing skill, her passion, and her wealth of experience, and transformed what I wanted to say into something that people wanted to read. Alison Jones was my mentor before she became my publisher. She 'got' the material and the book right from the start and her warmth, insight, and willingness to challenge have held me throughout the journey.

Isobel Ripley appeared just at the moment I needed her. She brought her humour, grace, courage, and remarkable emotional wisdom, and accompanied me in the endless edits. It's been such a delight to spend time with you Izzy, and I am looking forward to more collaboration.

I could write a whole chapter about Rachel Garstang, my best friend. Her warmth, empathy, humour, and unstinting support have carried me all the way – she read draft after draft and was always there at short notice for emergency moments. But the story that best sums up our relationship was the morning she told me that if I went under a bus today, it was fine; she now had enough material to be able to publish the book for me posthumously.

Dorothy Nesbit has offered countless hours of support, love, and wisdom. Dorothy, thank you particularly for bringing your eye for the bigger picture, your rock solid presence and your intelligence, care, and warmth. Deepening my friendship with you has been one of the biggest spin-off bonuses of this whole process.

Fi Macmillan, Maya Gudka, and Dorothy Martin were all there at the start. They encouraged me to get this book out of my head and onto paper and weren't afraid to ask the difficult questions. Clare Palmer and Laura Harvey helped me on the structure of the book and the first draft of early chapters. Clare's encouragement and constructive criticism reassured me hugely; Laura offered support just when I needed it, along with much-needed laughter and virtual wine.

Once I'd finished the first draft, we started with the heavy work of reading, editing, and rewriting. Debbie Redfern was my very first 'new to the subject' reader. Debbie, your response to the book gave me welcome early confirmation that it could have wide appeal. Thank you for your encouragement, enthusiasm, helpful commentary, and total reliability – all gold dust for me. Natasha Broke was a later addition to the team and made up for lost time by reading and commenting with such care and depth. Natasha was part of birthing my real live daughter, and it's been a joy to have you helping me birth my book. Thank you.

I loved sharing 'work' conversations with Jonathan Parr, and several of the illustration and metaphor ideas came straight from talking with him. I share Needs Understanding more effectively because of the impact that his creativity, kindness, and courage have had on me. Heather Monro is one of those who first put the idea of a book into my head. She has jumped in at key moments, bringing her razor-sharp intellect, intuitive understanding, gentle challenge, and willingness to go to difficult places. Mona Jeffreys, Suzy Andricopoulos, Gabriele Grunt, Catherine Weetman, Veronica Munro, Louise Wiles, Helen Beedham, and Fi Macmillan all read and commented on the draft manuscript, and each of you inspired changes which have made the book better.

As the work on the text was drawing to an end, the illustration team swept in. Lily Horseman drew the figures throughout. With patience, humour, and wonderful skill, she created characters who embody everything this book is about. Eduardo Iturralde designed the graphics and digitally remastered Lily's small people, and he is also responsible for creating the cover. His eye for spacing and impact is exactly what I wanted for this book, and he helped me with encouragement and support when I got very stuck. I am deeply grateful to you both for your part in shaping the beautiful finished product that we have, and thank you to Francesca (Froo) Signore and Roz Adams for putting me on to Lily and Eduardo in the first place.

As I write, I'm delighted to be in the process of meeting the team who are behind the production and post-production work on this book. Alongside Alison Jones, the team at Practical Inspiration Publishing and their production and design partners Newgen Publishing UK, particularly Shell Cooper, Michelle Charman, Judith Wise, and Sophie Robinson, have given me confidence that I'm in the best of hands.

It turns out that creating a book was a surprisingly emotional process for me, with some large mountains to climb. Sarah Heydon, Corrie Bell, Rebecca Crossthwaite, Cathy Swift, Helen O'Grady, Sophie Khan, and Bonnie Williams were an amazing support team, always there to encourage, understand and offer just the right advice. They came and climbed beside me when the pathway was obscured and the way ahead was steep, cheering me on with kindness and love. And throughout the journey, the authors group set up by Catherine Weetman provided writing direction, advice, and support. Thank you Catherine, Veronica Munro, Louise Wiles, and Ken Dickson for many a wise word and inspirational thought exchanged over Zoom.

Four people are central to my being alive and well today: Mark Collins, Lesley Kendrick, Cheryl Garner, and Christophe Edwards. Without any one of you this book would not exist, and it's quite possible that I wouldn't either. You gave me the gift of a second chance at life, and I've thrived because of you. The amazing Skyros family has also been key to what's been possible for me with this book. Among them are those with whom I've had particular connection: Fiona Buckle, Tracy Argent, Christine Schulz, Rhona Donaldson, Michelle Parker, Lottie Stockdale, Emma Crane, Malcolm Stern, Marianna Asimenou, and Gabriela Poulimenou.

There are so many others who have played a part in my recent story. It feels almost impossible to meaningfully pick out names, and still there are a few I want to mention, without this being anywhere near a complete list. Thank you all for your part in my journey: Penny Vine, Jo McHale, Penny Spawforth, Gayano Shaw, Graham Timmins, Roz Adams, Justyna Sokolowska, Gabriele Grunt, Sophie Docker, Emily and Barry Allsop, Sarah, Nick, Tom, and Katy Gwilliam, Jenny Shellens, Lara Montgomery, Mona Jeffreys, Sam Brightwell, Pavli, Ned, Eliška, and Minka Minns, Delphine Colin de Verdière, Matt Wait and Mark Pilkington, Edwina Macbeth, Hannah Reynolds, William and Luke Sheldon, Ben and George Parr, Abi Spence, Sallie Wood, Katie McMahon, Bella McMahon, Martha Redfern, Imogen Spence, and Alys Wood.

My brother, Ed Sheldon, has jumped in immediately every time I've turned to him for advice. He's always been ready to give me honest feedback about the book with love and understanding, and throughout my journey has never stopped believing in me. Robin Knowles has an inspiring passion for creating a fairer world, and has always supported me in my own efforts to bring about social change. He has contributed hugely to my own work over the years. My cousin Fiona Macbeth is the big sister that I never had – wise, inspiring, and warm. She's long been my role model for living a life of integrity, courage and love.

My parents are an enormous influence on my work. My father was warm and generous, and he loved people. My mother is strong and adventurous, and has always been there for me. Both have supported me throughout my life.

This book is dedicated to my daughter, whose love, beauty, and brightness bring me so much joy and delight. You have contributed to this book in so very many ways, and being your mum is the greatest privilege I will ever know.

Index of Pause Boxes

Index